ALTERNATIVES TO THE PEACE CORPS

"It was dark when the yellow Coope bus rolled into Agua Buena, Costa Rica. The main road—the only road—was dimly lit by flickering sodium lights that lined the small park to the south. As the bus slowed for the oncoming potholes, I caught my first glimpse of Don Roberto waiting by the bus stop and my first sight of Agua Buena. As he signaled to the driver to stop the bus, I grabbed my bag. It was my stop and the beginning of a journey, the full scope of which I could not appreciate at that moment.

The next six months I lived and worked with Roberto in the community of Agua Buena. We rose at dawn to work on the farm, shared stories over coffee and arroz con leche, talked town gossip around the coffee plants during harvest, and shared the ups and downs of life together. I am forever grateful for the genuine friendship that developed through this experience.

I worked in the coffee farms that dotted the hillsides, the small greenhouses, and the modest cooperative office. I would come to meet and build strong relationships with the farmers and residents of this small town and develop an understanding of the history and the environment of this region."

—Ian Bailey, Community Agroecology Network, Costa Rica

Alternatives t

FOOD FIRST BOOKS   OAKLAND, CALIFORNIA USA

the Peace Corps

A Guide to Global Volunteer Opportunities

TWELFTH EDITION

Edited by Caitlin Hachmyer

Food First Books
398 60th Street
Oakland, California 94618-1212
(510) 654-4400
www.foodfirst.org

Cover and text design: Amy Evans McClure
Cover photograph: Ian Bailey, Community Agroecology Network, Costa Rica
Photographs: p. iii, courtesy of Ian Bailey, Community Agroecology Network, Costa
Rica; pp. iv–v, courtesy of Voluntary Service Overseas (VSO) Canada; p. 1, courtesy
of Amizade, Ltd.; p. 35, courtesy of Global Vision International

Twelfth edition, 2008

CIP data on file with publisher
ISBN-10: 0-935028-31-5
ISBN-13: 978-0-935028-31-7
ISSN: 1541-2970

Food First Books are distributed by:
Perseus Distribution
387 Park Avenue South
New York, NY 10016
www.perseusdistribution.com

Printed in Canada

5 4 3 2 1

Contents

Acknowledgments

A LTERNATIVES TO THE PEACE CORPS has been developed
in response to the numerous inquiries Food First receives
from individuals seeking opportunities to gain community
development experience.

Becky Buell, a staff member at Food First from 1985 to 1988,
researched and wrote the original edition in 1986 with the
assistance of Kari Hamerschlag, a Food First intern. Tremendous demand for the book has created a continuing need to
revise and update it. Caitlin Hachmyer updated and expanded
the listing of volunteer opportunities for this twelfth edition,
with many thanks to the Food First staff — Martha Katigbak-
Fernandez for copyediting, Marilyn Borchardt for guidance,
Rowena Garcia for support, and Eric Holt-Giménez for perseverance. Special appreciation goes to fellow interns Devon
Sampson, Ian Bailey, Joey Smith, Meghan Holmes, Rachel
Fields, and Leonor Hurtado for their constant support and
friendship.

This book is made possible by the organizations, volunteers,
and friends that provide updates and additions. Much grati-
tude goes to the returned Peace Corps volunteers who have
offered their perspectives in the development of this guide.

Preface

HISTORICALLY, SOCIAL CHANGE HAS COME ABOUT THROUGH the tireless volunteer efforts of men and women working together in social movements. The 17th-century antislavery movement, women's emancipation, Gandhi's nonviolent satyagraha movement, the US's civil rights and free speech movement, the worldwide antiapartheid movement, and, more recently, the immigrant rights movement, the Campesino a Campesino movement, and the Landless Worker's Movement, to name only a few, all rely on thousands of people freely advocating for a just cause.

Just as important as frontline advocacy are the dedicated actions of the social practitioners who put these values into practice. It is never enough simply to advocate, to pass laws, or to change regulations. Peace, justice, dignity, and environmental sustainability must find their way into social practice in order to become a part of everyday life. To this end, there are thousands of service organizations carrying out work in communities and neighborhoods. They help local populations develop sustainable agriculture, improve community health, engage in popular education, and ensure respect for human rights. They fill out the normative frameworks by building alternatives on the ground. As with the advocacy of social change, volunteers play an extensive role in forging the practice of these social changes.

Alternatives to the Peace Corps is a guide to organizations that join practice with advocacy. Why alternatives? Because, even though the Peace Corps has recruited many fine volunteers over the years, it has been severely criticized for advancing US geopolitical and economic interests over the interests of the very people it is supposed to serve.

Since the Kennedy era, two generations of Americans have grown up supporting civil rights at home and seeking change in American foreign policy toward Vietnam, El Salvador, Nicaragua, South Africa, the Middle East, and a host of other regions. Many believe that US foreign policy has not always been helpful in building more equitable societies in nations of the global south. Neither human rights nor sustainable development has been the first priority of US foreign aid.

At Food First, we research world hunger extensively. Our analyses lead us to conclude that hunger is not caused by overpopulation, scarcity of food, or a lack of capability among impoverished people. It is caused by an unequal system of food production and distribution that enriches a small segment of society. Because of these inequalities, we emphasize the role of volunteers as participants in social change that is designed by and for local people.

Food First published the first edition of *Alternatives to the Peace Corps* in 1986 as a response to frequent requests for guidance on international volunteer opportunities that had no, or minimal, government strings attached. *Alternatives to the Peace Corps* was the first guide of its kind that offered options for voluntary service with private agencies that emphasized social change. The organizations and programs listed here seek volunteers who are interested in learning about local culture and desire to support efforts by local grassroots organizations.

Another important priority in publishing *Alternatives to the Peace Corps* is to help place volunteers with agencies working for social and political reform within the US. Hunger and poverty are not just foreign problems; here in America one in five children is growing up in poverty. The gap between rich and poor is increasing, creating a large underclass. Americans have always had a tradition of volunteer work. Volunteerism has supported many of our community-based organizations, from parent-school groups and the YMCA/YWCA to coalitions against homelessness. Dedicated volunteers for grassroots initiatives are needed more than ever today to counteract government cuts in programs for the disadvantaged, the elderly, immigrants, and the poor.

This twelfth edition of *Alternatives to the Peace Corps* is dedicated to the men and women, young and old, who want to share their talents with humanity to make this a better world.

Alternatives to the Peace Corps

PART I

Moving Beyond
the Peace Corps

Deciding how to volunteer is difficult. Knowing your reasons for wanting to volunteer is the first step toward choosing from among a huge variety of options: where to go, with what organization, and with what funds. A common solution to this conundrum is to choose a government-sponsored volunteer program, such as the US Peace Corps, with all expenses paid, plus training, health and accident insurance, travel expenses, and even a stipend. Serving with a government agency may also seem inherently safer than traveling thousands of miles from home under the auspices of a tiny nongovernmental organization (NGO) working for social change. And the Peace Corps name commands a level of recognition and respect that less well-known groups are hard-pressed to match.

This solution may seem simple enough. However, the Peace Corps and programs like it are not always as straightforward as they seem. The countries in which an agency works, the projects it supports, and the role of its volunteers have many underlying political, social, and cultural implications. Peace Corps volunteers are more than just well-intentioned individuals—they represent the governmental, religious, or institutional values and objectives of the organization that sponsors them.

Because the Peace Corps is an agency of the US government, the Peace Corps volunteer is part of the national team dispatched by the US State Department and is accountable to the US ambassador in the host country. The Peace Corps is inevitably linked to US foreign policy objectives, as is the Peace Corps volunteer.

The Peace Corps was founded by President John F. Kennedy to build America's positive image both at home and overseas during the Cold War. In his 1961 inaugural address, Kennedy challenged young Americans to join "a grand and global alliance . . . to fight tyranny, poverty, disease, and war. . . ." The Peace Corps was ostensibly an apolitical organization, but its image was tainted from the outset by underlying foreign policy agendas. One initial goal of the Peace Corps was to counter Soviet cultural and political influence in the global south; it was one tool used by the administration to eliminate the perceived threat of communism and to promote capitalism abroad.

The role of the Peace Corps in this agenda of the US government was no secret in its early years. A 1962 national security action memorandum signed by Kennedy ordered the directors of the CIA, the United States Agency for International Development (USAID), and the Peace Corps to "give utmost attention and emphasis to programs designed to counter Communist indirect aggression [through] . . . support of local police forces for internal security and counterinsurgency purposes." Because the Peace Corps was closely linked to the CIA during its first decade, it lost credibility in some countries.

Prodded by a Senate committee investigating intelligence agencies in 1977, the CIA reported that it had not used the Peace Corps as a cover for its operations since 1975. The assertion may have been intended as reassurance, but it raises concerns about what those operations were and whether they continue today under a different dispensation. In fact, more recently in 2003, the Russian government ended an 11-year contract with the Peace Corps, accusing Peace Corps volunteers of attempting to gather information about Russian officials.

Although these accusations were dismissed by the Peace Corps, they highlight a history of questionable Peace Corps connections to the CIA and of touchy relations between the US and Russia. As we will explore further, the Peace Corps still has strong ties to the US government's foreign policy interests and is far from an apolitical organization.

The ideological underpinnings of the Peace Corps reflect the changing nature and objectives of US foreign policy over time. By the 1990s, US foreign policy was no longer defined primarily by the military influence of the Cold War but by its ability to mold societies through economic intervention. By influencing the patterns of resource control, legislation, and monetary policy within the global south—whether through the International Monetary Fund (IMF) and World Bank's imposed structural adjustment programs or through free trade policies implemented by the World Trade Organization (WTO), the North American Free Trade Agreement (NAFTA), the Central American Free Trade Agreement (CAFTA), and bilateral trade agreements—the US government has found new ways to keep the global south safe for its brand of capitalism.

The Peace Corps reflected this shift beginning in the 1980s. Under the leadership of director Loret Miller Ruppe during the Reagan administration, the Peace Corps began billing itself less as a symbol of goodwill and more seriously as a so-called development agency. For example, agricultural and rural development is an area where this shift is evident. Through initiatives such as the African Food System Initiative and the Competitive Enterprise Development Program, Peace Corps volunteers began promoting private enterprise and the development of export production in the rural sector.

The development of these programs coincided with economic policies handed down from the IMF and World Bank. Together, these have effectively pushed poor farmers away from growing basic food crops and toward planting specialty crops for foreign markets. This is economically risky and environmentally unsound, often resulting in farmers falling irretrievably into debt as they start planting for export and eventually lose their land. Many impoverished countries now import basic grains and legumes that were available locally and in great variety before. The net impact of these changes has eroded the standing of poor farmers and has contributed to the spread of hunger. As representatives of the US Government, Peace Corps volunteers in some countries abetted this agricultural shift despite their benevolent intentions.

This example of agricultural development points to a recurring theme in the history of the Peace Corps. While the stated goals of the Peace Corps and the intentions of Peace Corps volunteers are for the betterment of the world community, they are consistently undermined by US policies that perpetuate economic disparities and human rights abuses, as well as hinder development for poor communities. Former President John F. Kennedy established the Peace Corps "to promote world peace and friendship." While Peace Corps volunteers are stationed across six continents, the US government leads the world in weapons sales and military training to countries *within* these continents (including Colombia, the Philippines, Pakistan, and Uzbekistan), and the US is one of the major advocates of IMF and World Bank structural adjustment programs. These policies promote neither peace nor friendship with the nations of the global south, and as an instrument of US policy, the Peace Corps cannot escape being tainted by them.

Another example of well-intended Peace Corps projects coinciding with damaging US policies is the role volunteers often take as teachers. Peace Corps volunteers are assigned to teach a wide array of subjects in nations of the global south, from math to HIV/AIDS awareness. While these volunteers are devoting their time and energy to education, however, other US policies are harming the educational systems in the very same countries. US-backed IMF and World Bank structural adjustment programs (required for nations to renegotiate their foreign debt) often require the governments of these nations to cut education budgets. US taxpayers pay about $80,000 for the training and service of each Peace Corps volunteer. That amount of money could pay the salaries of 40 or more local teachers in many of the countries where the Peace Corps runs programs.

The argument is often made that the Peace Corps simply goes where it is invited and does what it is asked to do. That is true, up to a point. But the projects the agency is willing to engage in and the numbers of volunteers it is willing to send— both with an eye to geopolitical interest—also enter into the equation. Foreign governments, not grassroots organizations, submit the requests for volunteers, and there is no guarantee that they have their citizens' best interests at heart. While on the one hand the US often expresses concern regarding the unstable nature of foreign governments, on the other hand we are trusting them to engage our citizens in what we are led to believe are the most deserving and appropriate programs for their people.

US foreign policy and the US government's goals for the Peace Corps took a new turn following September 11, 2001. In an effort to counter anti-American sentiment around the globe and particularly in the Middle East, President George W. Bush called for Americans to make a renewed commitment to volunteerism. In his 2002 State of the Union address, Bush unveiled the USA Freedom Corps, an umbrella organization to include the Peace Corps, AmeriCorps, and the Senior Corps, as well as a new Citizen Corps, whose purpose is to focus on the prevention of and emergency response to terrorism. President Bush called for the Peace Corps to double in size by 2007 and to expand its mission "to go into the Islamic world to spread the message of economic development and really share the compassion of a great nation." Oddly, in the subsequent years, "compassion" has coincided with a violent occupation of the Islamic world, resulting in an untold number of deaths—tens, if not hundreds of thousands. Further, being openly cited by the Bush administration as a tool in the fight to "overcome evil," the Peace Corps' mission has become undeniably repoliticized as part of this post-9/11 War on Terrorism. In fact, Bush frequently blends his messages about terrorism with a call to public service. Although increased volunteerism is a noble request at a time when the world needs people working for positive change, the president's motives are made questionable by the fact that his calls for American service across the globe are accompanied by the dismantling and defunding of a myriad of social programs in both the US and abroad, from sex education to affordable health care.

One Peace Corps volunteer's response to the new Freedom Corps illuminates some of these contradictions. This volunteer, serving in the Ivory Coast, criticized Bush's proposal to double the size of the Peace Corps because "it wouldn't do much to alleviate the poverty and hopelessness that foster terrorism. For, in reality, the Peace Corps does more to make us Americans feel good about ourselves than it does to fight poverty. Instead, we need to change the economic policies that I often find are punishing the very villagers I am trying to help." The volunteer cited the farm subsidy bill signed by Bush in May 2002, which increased subsidies to US cotton growers while African cotton farmers have to sell their cotton in a market depressed partly by overproduction in the US. "Expanding the Peace Corps is a nice gesture. But if that's the sort of carrot we're using alongside the very big stick of US economic and military might, it isn't much of a meal. . . . What we really need to do is fill the stomachs and pocketbooks of nations of the global south."

If the Peace Corps is serious about its goal of capacity-building (in development lingo, imparting skills and knowledge rather than simply performing charity), then the Peace Corps may assist host nations right out of their need for the Peace Corps. This should not be considered a bad thing.

Volunteering for the Peace Corps

Many Peace Corps volunteers would argue that their placement had little or nothing to do with the larger policy objectives of

Structural Adjustment

During the 1980s and 1990s international agencies including the IMF and the World Bank forced structural changes on economies in the global south. Loans desperately needed to restructure foreign debts were conditioned on the performance of structural adjustment programs—technocratic plans with the declared aim of making economies more efficient, competitive, and capable of growth. In fact, a principal effect, and perhaps even aim, of these programs has been to pry open the economies of nations of the global south for foreign corporations, providing them with new markets and investment opportunities. This has been accomplished by imposing diverse free market policies, including privatizing state enterprises, deregulating (removal of restrictions on investment, both domestic and foreign), slashing of government budgets for health, education, and social services, and removing import barriers. In country after country, the impact of these adjustments on the living conditions of the majority has been disastrous. Carried out on a large scale and in a very short time span, privatization transferred the benefits of institutions and resources from the general public to private businesses. In most countries, the gap between rich and poor widened as economic power became more sharply concentrated in increasingly fewer hands. As a result, poverty and hunger escalated in the global south during the 1980s and early 1990s, especially in Latin America and Africa, where "adjustment" was more assiduously implemented by local elites. The IMF and World Bank continue to loan conditionally to nations in the south. However, the IMF no longer refers to these as "structural adjustment" policies. In 1999, the IMF replaced the Enhanced Structural Adjustment Facility with the Poverty Reduction and Growth Facility, although the function is essentially the same.

(**Source:** *World Hunger: Twelve Myths*, by Frances Moore Lappé, Joseph Collins, and Peter Rosset, 1999, p. 103.)

the US government. One volunteer working in a mountain region of the Philippines had no contact with the Peace Corps office, USAID, or any other Peace Corps volunteer in his two years of service. "I arrived at the community and worked out my role with them," he explained. Most volunteers believe that their service had a positive impact, independent of the other agencies and policy initiatives of the US government. "I worked with women to develop composting techniques and planting vegetables," said a volunteer working in Honduras. "These are techniques that will benefit them for a lifetime."

Despite the fact that some Peace Corps volunteers have felt their work was autonomous from US government policy, the link is inherent, and federal lawmakers have referred to the connection as a matter of course. "If there is a person in the Peace Corps who feels he cannot support US foreign policy, then he ought not to be in the Peace Corps," stated Senator Ross Adair (R-Ind). Loret Miller Ruppe, director of the Peace Corps for eight years, proclaimed proudly at the outset of her tenure in 1981 that she hoped to prove her agency's work "a valuable source of real aid to US foreign policy."

In general, the Peace Corps discourages expressions of dissent from federal doctrine. During the Vietnam War, the Peace Corps stipulated that no public disapproval of the war would be tolerated, and in a widely publicized incident, a volunteer in Chile was dismissed after he wrote a letter denouncing the war to a Chilean newspaper. Yet even keeping one's views silent and working diligently to encourage real development may not be a sufficient shield from policy imperatives. A pair of volunteers in Honduras in the 1980s were commanded to "name the names" of local citizens that their sector boss believed were communists. Prospective volunteers should think carefully about how their political views may be inhibited by their placement with the Peace Corps.

Other criticisms have been leveled at the Peace Corps over the years. Former volunteers and staff have accused the agency of providing insufficient training, of defining goals and tasks too vaguely, and of withholding follow-through, thus hindering the long-term sustainability of projects. Additionally, returnees note that the Peace Corps often uses the presence or number of volunteers sent as a bargaining chip in its relations with countries. For instance during the 1980s Central American nations that allied with the US were flooded with volunteers to counterbalance the heightened US military presence there and to put a good face on the US-backed intervention against Sandinista Nicaragua.

Despite all the concerns about the Peace Corps as an arm of US foreign policy marked by these examples, the agency must be credited with enabling thousands of American citizens to witness the realities of poverty and injustice in the global south. The refrain one hears over and over again in statements from returned volunteers is, "I got much more than I gave." Most Peace Corps volunteers will attest that living and working alongside people in poor communities was the most powerful experience of their lives—one that has influenced their decisions and actions ever since. Many returned Peace Corps volunteers have learned through their placement about the intimate connections between development and economic justice, militarization and human rights. They return to the US and work to make US foreign and domestic policy more accountable to the poor.

As one returned Peace Corps volunteer explained, "If there is one thing to thank the Peace Corps for, it's for showing me how US policies hurt the average person. In a country like Paraguay, it is hard to miss the connection between US aid and the oppression of the poor. It is hard to miss the links between the IMF economic package and the inability of the poor to feed themselves. These realizations radically changed my perspectives on the world." However, as will later become clear, the Peace Corps is not the only way to have such valuable experiences.

United States Agency for International Development

A look at some of the other federal agencies involved in development work is in order. The US Agency for International Development (USAID), created by President Kennedy in 1961, the same year as the Peace Corps, states frankly on its website that the purpose of US aid to other nations is to further America's foreign policy interests. Through field offices in foreign countries, USAID funnels monetary aid and technical assistance to projects that are in keeping with the purposes of foreign policy. Many of these projects have involved leaning on governments to privatize state-owned industries, allow greater foreign investment, and decrease spending on social programs such as health, education, and food subsidies. USAID has helped to uphold the regime of debt service imposed upon many poor countries by the IMF and the World Bank, and to enforce the claims of US corporations conducting business abroad. Too often, the agency has pushed for costly solutions to local problems, and its projects have enriched only the wealthiest citizens of nations in the global south. For these reasons, in this guide, we have tried to avoid listing organizations that accept money from USAID.

Other National Service Programs
VISTA, the Corporation for National and Community Service, and the USA Freedom Corps

The government volunteer service program in the US, now known as the Corporation for National and Community Service, offers another interesting comparison to the Peace Corps. In 1964, President Johnson created VISTA (Volunteers in Service to America) as the "domestic Peace Corps." Then in 1993, under President Clinton, VISTA became a part of the newly created Americorps, a domestic aid program encompassed by the Corporation for National and Community Service along with the Senior Corps and Learn and Serve America. The purpose of these programs was, and is, to address issues such as homeless-ness, illiteracy, and economic and neighborhood revitalization through placements with nonprofits, public agencies, and faith-based organizations. As with the Peace Corps, volunteers are prohibited from engaging in political activity during their par-ticipation, and there can be little doubt that the stated aims of the projects AmeriCorps (and VISTA before it) supports sel-dom run counter to official US policy on poverty. Yet, in its early years, VISTA's emphasis on community organizing and self-help over service delivery—as well as its removal from the realm of foreign relations and the imperative of upholding our image overseas—garnered the agency a reputation for activism, even radicalism. VISTA promoted welfare reform legislation and later assisted with its implementation, which actually under-mined VISTA's goal of reducing poverty. Over the years, VISTA gradually shifted its focus away from remedying poverty toward more general service endeavors; it promoted volunteerism less as an agent of social change and more as a salutary and fulfill-ing activity for concerned citizens. Like USAID and the Peace Corps, its first concern is the proper placement and use of the aid giver, not the long-term needs of the aid receiver.

President Bush realigned AmeriCorps with domestic and foreign federal policies in 2002 when, after 9/11, he created the USA Freedom Corps, an organization promoting serv-ice opportunities in America. He asked for the expansion of AmeriCorps to assist with homeland security and the War on Terrorism and created Citizen Corps, an organization working with both the Department of Homeland Security and the Corporation for National and Community Service, aimed to engage citizens with issues of homeland security and commu-nity safety and preparedness. The Citizens Service Act that described this expansion also included changes to the pledge taken by AmeriCorps volunteers. Previously the pledge focused on community service, made no mention of the US Consti-tution, and had no religious references. In this bill, however, officials proposed a new pledge in which volunteers would

promise to support the Constitution of the US "in God's name."
This pledge would be voluntary, but clearly there is a push in
Washington for increased political and religious influence on
AmeriCorps public service programs.

Nongovernmental Organizations

Much has been said and written over the last two decades about
the proliferation of nongovernmental organizations throughout the world and their potential for enacting social and political change. In countries of the global south and the global north
the last 20 years have witnessed a massive upsurge in the number of citizens' organizations airing grievances, lobbying for
redress, mobilizing protests, establishing needed services for
their constituents, and advocating for democratization of the
forces of market and state. Concurrent has been the rise of
resource or support organizations, often, but not exclusively, in
the north, that provide research, advice, information, grants, or
other aid to citizens' groups or to broader movements. In the
north, both kinds of groups are generally referred to as NGOs,
"civil society," the "voluntary sector," or "third sector" (as in a
sector separate from both the market and the state). In the US,
NGOs are often referred to as "nonprofits." Many in the global
south distinguish between NGOs, which offer research and
support, and civil society groups or social movements, which
have a popular base. Lester Salamon, director of the Institute
for Policy Studies at Johns Hopkins University, has used the
term "associational revolution" to describe the growing size and
strength of civil society groups of all kinds. Their appeal to
believers throughout the political spectrum is considerable, and
their successes have inspired much optimism that they can
accomplish what market and state have failed to bring about.
To name just one example, concerted networking among hundreds of civil society organizations put thousands of protesters
on the streets of Seattle during the WTO's Third Ministerial
Conference in 1999. This was the start of a growing global

movement for economic and social justice, manifested in the streets of cities all over the world in recent years.

Choices outside of the Peace Corps are important because they provide volunteer options for those given pause by the often unrealized history and agenda behind the government-affiliated organizations described above. In the same way that the more diverse an ecosystem is the richer that ecosystem will be, a diversified network of ideas and methods is the richest and most productive way to address a problem. Options create the opportunity to incorporate all the various strengths that individuals bring to the world and to bring them together in different combinations to address the diverse problems that are faced around the globe. It would seem that the more diverse the projects and ideas are, the more likely it is that successful and sustainable solutions will be realized. Additionally, this diversification maintains a system of checks and balances, in which no single organization holds a monopoly over the analysis, decision-making, and problem-solving methods related to a range of global issues.

However, the emphasis on third-sector solutions can conceal a retreat from necessary government-supported solutions to poverty and injustice, such as agrarian reform or income redistribution. In the present day, when 53 of the 100 largest economies in the world are transnational corporations, one cannot be too complacent about the strength of the market or the role governments play in enforcing inequalities of wealth. The presence of the third sector in and of itself is not a cure for social problems. It is a powerful tool, but only one tool among several.

The future of nongovernmental organizations and social movements appears promising. These days USAID and the Peace Corps employ the rhetoric of "grassroots empowerment" and "local decision making" in describing their own projects. We welcome this sign of the trickling up of NGO influence and can only hope that there is sufficient substance behind the words to make a real difference in some people's lives.

The organizations in this book are, or work in cooperation with, NGOs and citizens' groups—not the government—in countries receiving volunteers. International cooperation among these groups is no guarantee against wasted or misguided efforts, but at least the work that gets accomplished is much less likely to be confused with, or compromised by, the agendas of government, either ours or someone else's. Readers of this book are encouraged to involve themselves in truly sustainable development. International cooperation can be built most effectively through the empowerment and leadership of local people.

2

ASSESSING YOUR NEEDS AND
NARROWING YOUR SEARCH

CHOOSING A VOLUNTEER PROGRAM INVOLVES ASSESS-
ing your own ideals and personal needs and then finding
an organization or program that matches those best. You may
know that you want to work with children or on sustainable
development, or that you want to work with an organization
that is completely run by local people rather than one that is
based in the US or Europe. You may have only a month to volunteer or financial constraints that affect the type of program
you are able to do. It is important to know the different possibilities and their strengths and weaknesses in order to match
your needs.

What Sorts of Projects Are Available?

In a few pages, we'll get to assessing your own needs and options
and evaluating organizations. First let's take a look at the types
of opportunities that are available, and what their benefits and
drawbacks might be.

Long-Term Projects

The Peace Corps requires a two-year commitment from its volunteers. Whether you are planning to volunteer in Zimbabwe or in Arizona, the more time you spend there, the better you will understand the community and the more you will be able to contribute. In the first months of your volunteer experience, you will mostly be learning from the people you are working with. It takes a long time before you develop the knowledge and connections necessary to even begin to contribute. Drawbacks of this kind of commitment are obvious—a long-term, intensive experience is not for everyone. You may have other financial or time commitments, or responsibilities, that keep you from volunteering for a year or more. And, if you are not going through an organization that offers a living stipend, you may worry about how you can support yourself as a volunteer for such a long time. If this is the case, read the section on fundraising in this chapter for some suggestions for making a long-term volunteer commitment financially possible.

Short-Term Opportunities

While some organizations require a minimum six-month or one-year commitment from volunteers, you may not have the freedom to spend more than a month volunteering. Some of the organizations listed in the "International" and "US" sections of this book run shorter programs that focus on cultural exchange, as well as service projects to benefit the community you are visiting. Be aware that a shorter-term commitment will probably end up being more of a cultural exchange, and an excellent educational experience for you, than a chance to see a substantial service project through. However, a well-run program offering shorter-term volunteer slots can still be of genuine service to a local community.

Alternative Travel

If your time is limited, you may also want to look into socially responsible trips and tours. Several organizations and travel agencies lead "reality tours" abroad. These are socially responsible educational tours that provide participants with firsthand experience of the political, economic, and social structures that create or promote hunger, poverty, and environmental degradation. Tours offer an opportunity to meet people with diverse perspectives on agriculture, development, and the environment. They often include the opportunity to stay with local people, visit rural areas, and meet with grassroots organizers. Such tours can alter your understanding of hunger and poverty and direct you to areas where you can best work for democratic social change. These are great opportunities for people who need a shorter-term, intensive, and well-structured experience. However, these are not always the cheapest options and are usually more educational than service oriented.

Volunteering as a Student

A number of universities offer study-abroad programs that provide an opportunity to learn about the political, economic, and social conditions in a given country. Several of these programs are listed in the "Alternative Travel and Study Overseas" section of this book. It is possible, however, to combine almost any sort of overseas study program with volunteer work, if you are enterprising. Once established in a country, seek out individuals and groups directly involved with community development. They may be able to direct you to an appropriate volunteer placement where you can build your skills and experience in the field. Working in this way can give you the contacts, experience, and confidence you may need for a longer or more intensive overseas experience when you are finished with school.

Professional/Skilled Exchange

Many organizations welcome volunteers with specific technical skills in such fields as construction, health care, and agriculture. If you have some years of experience in a particular area, working directly with an organization or community that needs people with your experience is a great opportunity for you. Organizations that are focused on local, grassroots work will often only accept volunteers with very specific skills that the organization is lacking and needs to further its work. This kind of volunteer opportunity is probably one of the best ways to do truly effective work for a community. The closer your skills match their needs, and the more involved you can be on a practical level, the more productive your experience will be for both you and the community you are working in. In any work experience, local people can best define your role. Let them know what your skills are and allow them to decide how they can best put those skills to use.

Working Overseas

Most overseas development positions require two or more years of community development experience. While a two-year volunteer post does not guarantee future employment, you may find that by developing your skills and connections with communities in the developing world, job possibilities will open up. To guide you in your job search, you will find organizations and publications in the "Resources" section that list employment openings overseas.

Designing Your Own Experience

For someone who has significant travel experience and a solid focus on the kind of work he or she would like to do abroad, this may be the best option. It can be a wonderful experience to design your own trip and project, especially if you have a unique schedule or already know the area you are traveling to. Just remember that the longer you stay in a community, the greater the difference you can make. Most of the organizations we have listed in this book are based in the US or Europe and make international connections for their volunteers. However, there are thousands of NGOs, both small and large, all over the world, and we could not possibly include all of them here.

You can begin by researching grassroots organizations and contacting them to find out more about their needs and the types of skills they can use. When designing your own experience, it is important to think carefully about the specific skills you can bring to an organization and to be clear about what you can offer to the organizations you contact. A volunteer who went to work with a community organization in Mexico learned that his most useful skill was puppet making. He didn't know before he arrived that street theater is a popular form of political communication. When a local clinic learned that he was an artist and an actor, they suggested that he help them communicate health care information through puppet shows.

In the "Resources" section of this book, we have included several publications and websites that list NGOs and other volunteer opportunities. The Internet is an invaluable resource for finding organizations. After spending an hour or two searching, you will probably have several organizations to contact, and you can begin to narrow your search depending on the needs and values of each organization. While researching and making connections from home is essential, it may be that you need to wait until you are in country to figure out the details of your volunteer experience. Many small NGOs do not have Internet access, and you can only learn about them once you are there. The most important thing for you to do when you are working independently is to talk to people. The more people you meet and learn from, the more connections you will make and the more doors will open.

Keep in mind that it is a mistake to assume that all grassroots organizations need or want volunteers. Some groups are suspicious of the idea of unpaid labor in any context. Some emphasize the values of mutual aid and local empowerment to the point of not wanting volunteers from outside the community. Do not presume that, with a little coaxing or bargaining, you can overcome the resistance of someone who says no to your offer to volunteer. When you contact organizations, clearly state your goals, expectations, skills, and the length of time you are available. The organization can then decide if you can be of service in its work.

What Are Your Motivations?

Before committing to an organization, it is important to clarify your motives and your constraints. You may be drawn to voluntary service by a desire to help people striving for social, political, or economic change; you may be interested in learning about another culture and society; you may seek adventure; you may be eager to gain experience that will help you find a job. Your motivation may consist of all these reasons and more, to varying degrees. Thoroughly understanding why you want to volunteer can help you find the right organization, keep you focused and confident during your service, and ensure that you get the most from the experience.

Humanitarian motivations lead many prospective volunteers to communities plagued by extreme poverty and injustice. A volunteer may wish to feed the hungry, heal the sick, or house the homeless, but these social and political problems are often incredibly complex. Learning the dynamics of a community is the greatest challenge to a volunteer, making the volunteer's most appropriate role that of a student. An ill-advised motivation for volunteering can sometimes accompany the humanitarian impulse. This motivation might be called crusaderism —wanting to travel to far-flung pockets of deprivation and change everything in the space of three months. To expect too much from your volunteer experience is to set yourself up for disappointment. We might do well to heed the observation of Dorothy Day, cofounder of the Catholic Worker Movement in the 1930s, who assessed the slow pace of social change: "What we do is so little that we may seem to be constantly failing. . . . And why must we see the results of our giving? Our work is to sow—another generation will be reaping the harvest."

Concerned American citizens who want to help impoverished people don't need to travel around the globe to fulfill their goals. The challenges of community development here at home are immense. For this reason, one section of this book is dedicated to US organizations. Voluntary service in low-income communities in the US can also be a valuable educational experience or preparation for future work.

Another motivation for voluntary service is the desire to learn more about other societies. Living in another country can build your appreciation of the richness of other cultures and enable you to gain a comparative perspective on life in the US. Shorter-term experiences such as work brigades, study tours, and international education programs often offer a component of historical and theoretical insight into problems faced by the communities you visit. Many such programs are specifically designed for students. In this book, a number of tour, education, and shorter-term programs are also listed in the "Alternative Travel and Study Overseas" section.

If your concern is to improve your qualifications for a career in development, an unconventional work experience may enhance your candidacy. The best programs place volunteers with local NGOs that have requested a volunteer for a specific purpose. In these circumstances, volunteers have a better chance of making a meaningful contribution. These placements often require some skills—computer, teaching, agriculture, appropriate technology, health care, or fundraising. If you do not already have experience in these areas, it would be wise to develop specific technical skills that may be of use to an organization, as well as language competency.

Simple escapism—the desire to get away from home to evade personal problems or because you can't decide on a career—is an understandable impulse, but it's not the best motivation for volunteering. If you are troubled, preoccupied, or at loose ends, your effectiveness overseas will be diminished.

Evaluating an Organization

The listings in this book describe dozens of organizations that we think offer strong alternatives for overseas and domestic volunteer experiences. But the listings are just a start. In addition to this book, many resources are available for finding organizations on your own, such as the Internet, career counseling centers, your friends, and other books. A few ideas are listed in the "Resources" section at the back of this book. Take the time to explore the myriad of opportunities available, both in this book and beyond, to find the organization or project best suited to your needs, motivations, and skills.

No matter which voluntary service organization you are considering, it is important to ask questions that allow you to evaluate its motives, methods, and effectiveness. You want to be sure that the organization you devote your time and energy to is in line with your goals and values before you commit to working with them. To help you in this process, here are some questions based on those we used to evaluate the organizations included in this book. You may think of others that will help you match an organization's values to your own.

- What is the political or religious affiliation of the organization? Is its purpose to convert or influence people to adopt new cultural, economic, or social values?

- What is the organization's mission statement? How does it actually work to accomplish its goals?

- Will you be taking a job that could be done by a local person? If you are offering a new skill to an area, does the program involve transferring that skill to local people? Are the organization's goals to make the program self-sustainable?

- Who funds the organization? Do the funding sources have political or religious affiliations that may influence the organization's programs?

- How does the organization choose its programs? Have local people requested help from volunteers? Or do staff, funders, or the organization's board determine its programs?

- Is the organization working with local or national governments?

- If the organization says it works with local groups or NGOs, find out what types of groups they mean and what type of partnership they have. For example, the organization might work with a local school on an environmental education project or with a women's group working for economic self-sufficiency.

- What sort of training and support can you expect as a volunteer?

To answer questions like these, look beyond the program's brochures. If possible, get a list of previous volunteers and ask them about their experiences. Did they get good training and support? Was the experience what they expected based on the organization's claims, and, if not, why not? You may also want to write to people in the field, finding out who is critical of the program and why. To further understand the influences under which the organization may be working, find the most recent annual report on their website and read through the financial section. This will give you a list of their funding sources, further illuminating the motivations behind their work. Additionally, obtaining a copy of the organization's federal 990 forms, which can be found through GuideStar.org, a database of nonprofit organizations, will give you detailed financial information regarding how much money came into the organization and how funding was broken down into individual programs. Researching the organization's board members and their other affiliations is another way to learn about the underpinnings of an NGO. These things will help you more thoroughly assess your compatibility with the organization. The section called

"Further Reading" lists several books that take a critical look at development organizations overseas and is yet another source for your analysis.

Whether you decide on an organized volunteer program, a tour, or to go on your own, it is essential to do your homework beforehand. Read as much as possible about the geographic area (especially its history and politics), learn about groups working in the area, write in advance to groups that interest you, and talk to people at home who know about the area you are considering.

Fundraising

One of the biggest challenges that comes with choosing an alternative to the Peace Corps is finding a way to finance your trip. While some agencies offer a stipend, insurance, or travel expenses, many smaller programs are not able to offer these benefits. Government or church organizations can often afford to be more generous, and this is a major reason people choose to work through these organizations. Making your desire to work at the grassroots level a reality will require a creative approach to fundraising. If you choose to work with a small, local organization, it is highly unlikely that they will be able to help you with your expenses. Truthfully, they cannot afford to put their resources anywhere but directly into the community in which they are working.

The first thing you should do is come up with a tentative, itemized budget for your trip. Research the potential costs of each of your expenses before you begin fundraising. Not only does this give you a goal to reach in your fundraising efforts, it shows those you are asking that you have given thought to your budget and are asking for money you will actually need.

Below is a list of many of the items you should include:

- Transportation to and from the site (airline tickets are often the biggest expense for a trip to a nation where housing and food costs are minimal compared to the US)

- Program fee (consult the program you are interested in to find out what fee, if any, they require)

- Housing costs

- Food costs

- Transportation during your stay (buses, trains, etc.)

- Communication costs (stamps, phone cards, Internet fees)

- Spending money

- Medical insurance

- Visa fee

- Medicine

- Departure tax (from the airport abroad)

- Travel gear (this includes anything you may need to buy, such as mosquito nets, water filters, camping equipment, etc.)

- Passport application fee

- Other (e.g., student loan repayments or other obligations)

Airfare will be your primary expense. Living in a nation of the global south, especially in rural areas, is by and large extremely affordable in comparison to living in the US. If you can arrange an internship or a work exchange (like teaching English) for room and board, your living expenses can be kept to a minimum. Ask the organization you'll be working with for suggestions about this, though it will probably be easier to arrange a work exchange once you are in country. The best way to find out how much money you should expect to need for some of these items, such as transportation and spending money, is to ask people who have worked or lived in the area you are traveling to. Ask the organization you are going to work with and volunteers who have worked with the organization in the past about costs.

Once you have figured out an estimated budget, don't let the numbers daunt you! You can go about finding the funds to support your trip in several ways, and if you make a fundraising plan and stick to it, you are very likely to raise the funds you need. Your plan should include efforts to raise funds from several sources (some of which are described below). Approaching several sources in a thoughtful manner will bring success more quickly than putting all your eggs in one basket and hoping for the best. Successful fundraising requires equal parts research, creativity, perseverance, and willingness to ask for help.

Scholarships and Fellowships
These are often available through universities, and if you are enrolled in school, you should find out what resources are available for students wishing to travel to research or volunteer abroad. Universities also offer stipends toward room and board expenses for internships or volunteer programs in the US. Public libraries, career service centers, and specialized libraries like the Foundation Center—which has branches throughout the country—are sources for information on grants and loans. You may also be able to find funding through your local government, private associations, or church groups. For example, the Rotary Club offers scholarships for foreign travel, and many churches support their parishioners in return for educational services upon return from an overseas trip.

Loans and Gifts
Friends and relatives are another possible source of funds. You may be able to arrange a personal loan, or ask your extended circle for small contributions, using a well-written fundraising letter that describes your project and what you'll use the money for.

Events and Exchanges
Consider organizing a fundraising pancake breakfast, bake sale, or white-elephant sale. Friends, family, club or church mem-

bers, or local businesses may be willing to help you by donating time, space, food, services, or items for sale. One woman who traveled throughout Central America for a year started her own newsletter and asked friends and family to subscribe to help subsidize her living expenses. If you receive funding from individuals or organizations, your funders may appreciate a slide show or talk about your experiences upon your return—or, if you're inclined, start a weblog that will help them share your experiences as they happen.

Your Own Resources

One source of funds (maybe the main source) will be your own bank account. Part of your fundraising plan will probably include working for a while to save money for a trip or using savings you already have. You may also consider selling some possessions to help finance your travels.

Bringing the Lessons to Life

Working with poor communities, whether at home or abroad, to confront the causes of hunger and poverty can have a long-lasting impact on your life. It can deepen your understanding of the tremendous power the US has over the lives of people around the world: to make and break governments; to affect the world economy through trade, investment, and foreign aid policies; and to influence economic priorities through USAID, the World Bank, the International Monetary Fund, and the World Trade Organization, among other entities.

The lessons you learn may have direct applications: working to end hunger and poverty in the US, pressuring the US government to end its involvement with repressive regimes, limiting arms sales to nations in the global south, and holding US corporations accountable for their actions, whether overseas or at home.

An experience in a nation of the global south can be translated into work at home in many ways. A Peace Corps volunteer who served with Guatemalan Indians returned to the US and worked with Native Americans in Arizona. A health care volunteer with an international organization in Ghana found work at a free clinic in California. An agricultural extension worker who volunteered in Mozambique became active in the movement to stop US support of South Africa's apartheid regime. These examples and others show that experience in a marginalized community is often the catalyst for taking action in your own country to create more democratic organizations and politics at the local, national, and international levels, and to help ensure the survival of grassroots efforts all over the world.

3

How to Use This Book

IN COMPILING THE FOLLOWING LISTS OF ORGANIZATIONS, we looked for groups that address the political and economic causes of poverty. In our view, these programs place volunteers in positions that complement the work of local people, grassroots organizations, and nongovernmental organizations (NGOs) by focusing on capacity building and providing services that are sustainable.

We used several criteria when deciding which organizations to include in this book. Organizations that rely on US government funding are not included because government money can never be completely free from Washington's agendas. A command of the English language has become a desirable attainment in many countries in the global south, but we list none of the organizations that deal strictly in sending English teachers overseas. We include only a few of the organizations devoted to sending teachers abroad as part of their program, on the grounds that most English programs serve primarily the host countries' middle or professional classes. We have tried to steer clear of any organizations that are evangelical, but we do list some volunteer programs with religious affiliations that hold as their primary purpose the support of local community development efforts. Some do require a commitment to a certain faith, but most ask only that the volunteer share a concern for social justice. As with any volunteer placement, it is important to clearly understand the values behind an agency's volunteer program. We have done the initial screening, but you should investigate an organization thoroughly before you choose to work with them.

The listings are by no means comprehensive. Many organizations are so small and take so few volunteers that they prefer not to be listed, which is not to say that they would not like to be approached by informed and enterprising potential volunteers. Hundreds of other possibilities are not mentioned because they are so locally based that it makes more sense to find and contact them once you are abroad. We were only able to include a fraction of the organizations doing good work around the globe, so this book should be a launching point in your search for volunteer opportunities and commitment to social justice. Every community, school, church, and labor union has the potential for developing international programs that send delegates abroad, initiate ongoing partnership programs, and offer direct assistance to communities in the global south or underserved communities in the US. These opportunities are often the most exciting, but they must be created by the volunteer. (See the "Designing Your Own Experience" section in chapter 2, for more information.)

The organizations in this book are divided into four sections. The first two sections, "International Voluntary Service Organizations" and "US Voluntary Service Organizations," are self-explanatory. In the "Alternative Travel and Study Overseas" section, you'll find organizations that sponsor short-term work projects, educational travel to frequently inaccessible areas of the world, and opportunities to study abroad. The last section, "Resources," includes other organizations and guides that do not sponsor regular volunteer programs but may distribute information or serve as a resource in your search.

To aid you in using this guide and searching for the best volunteer opportunity for you, we have provided two indexes at the back of the book, one alphabetical and one geographical. If you are looking for a volunteer program in a specific region of the world, refer to the geographical index.

You will find icons beside the entries for many organizations included in this book to help you narrow your search quickly. The icons are meant to be a resource for you, but not a definitive word on any of these organizations. You should contact organizations directly with specific questions. A key for these icons appears below.

Key to Symbols

All of these organizations have a **religious affiliation**. Buddhism, Catholicism, and Judaism are just a few of the faith groups represented in this book. Some organizations are affiliated with a specific religious tradition, while others identify as interfaith. Most of these organizations do not require that their volunteers be of a certain faith, and the emphasis on religion varies greatly among these groups.

These organizations request **proficiency in a foreign language** for participation in some or all of their programs. While some of these organizations require fluency in a foreign language, some say knowledge of a foreign language is helpful, but not necessary.

These organizations offer some **short-term** volunteer opportunities of one month or less. (This icon does not appear in the "Alternative Travel and Study Overseas" section because most of the organizations listed in that section offer *only* short-term opportunities.)

These organizations all offer some kind of **financial assistance** to their volunteers. This ranges from groups that offer complete coverage of all expenses, including airfare, to organizations that provide modest monthly stipends abroad, to groups that offer a very limited number of scholarships.

Organizations and Resources

PART II

4

INTERNATIONAL VOLUNTARY SERVICE ORGANIZATIONS

THE FOLLOWING ORGANIZATIONS OFFER OPPORTUNITIES to work abroad on a wide variety of issues and projects. These voluntary service organizations are selected for their common approach to combating injustices, emphasizing support of grassroots efforts around the globe. They are building international cooperation through the empowerment and leadership of local people.

Agencia Latinoamericana de Información (ALAI)
12 de octubre N18-24 y Patria, Of 503, Quito, Ecuador
Mailing address: Casilla 17-12-877, Quito, Ecuador
Tel: + (593 2) 250-5074 *or* + (593 2) 222-1570
Fax: + (593 2) 250-5073
E-mail: info@alainet.org
Website: alainet.org

ALAI is a communications organization committed to human rights, gender equality, and people's participation in the development of Latin America. ALAI works for the democratization of communication. To that end, it has developed a model of alternative communication that aims toward the formation of a new fabric of communication that is democratic, widespread, decentralized, and multicultural.

ALAI accepts a few volunteers in its Quito office each year. Volunteers may assist with translation, journalism, or documentation work for ALAI's publications and website, or help design ALAI's website and databases. Volunteers are expected to cover their own expenses. ALAI welcomes applications from persons with disabilities, though no special facilities—other than elevator access to their office—exist.

Amazon-Africa Aid Organization (3AO)

PO Box 7776, Ann Arbor, MI 48107
Tel: (734) 769-5778
Fax: (734) 769-5779
E-mail: info@amazonafrica.org
Website: www.amazonafrica.org

3AO is a US nonprofit that partners with the Brazilian NGO Fundação Esperança to support the work of the Bill Chase Dental Clinic in the Brazilian Amazon. Located in the small city of Santarém, where the dark blue Tapajós waters flow into the muddy Amazon, the clinic provides necessary dental and other health care services to an impoverished mixed-race community undergoing rapid social change. For over 30 years Fundação Esperança has been providing health care and education to the people of the Amazon. In an average year, the clinic's dental team performs over 26,000 procedures, including restorations, extractions, root canals, and x-rays. 3AO seeks accredited medical doctors and dentists who are willing to volunteer two to six weeks of their time at the dental clinic. The clinic will accommodate spouses, who often teach English to staff and students. Volunteers are asked to cover the price of their airfare to Santarém, but 3AO pays for room and board.

American Friends Service Committee (AFSC)
International Programs   § 88 88

Volunteer Service
1501 Cherry Street, Philadelphia, PA 19102-1479
Fax: (215) 241-7026
Website: www.afsc.org
Mexico Summer Youth Project
Tel: (215) 241-7295
E-mail: mexicosummer@afsc.org
Website: www.afsc.org/mexicosummer.html
China Summer Work Camp
Website: www.pym.org/workcamp.China/china.htm

Mexico Summer Project, a seven-week project in Sierra Norte de Puebla, Mexico, strives to raise the consciousness of its participants, allowing them to become more aware of how an individual's personal experiences are connected to and affect larger societal problems and solutions. Youth from the Americas, Europe, and Mexico engage in sustainable development projects and cultural exchange workshops as a medium for learning. Participants must be mature individuals, 18–26 years old and able to communicate well in Spanish—the language of the project—at all times. The program runs from the end of June to mid-August. A project fee of $1,350 includes food, lodging, and project materials, but not travel expenses. Scholarships are possible for people with demonstrated financial need. The project is run in collaboration with Servicio, Desarrollo, y Paz A.C. (SEDEPAC), a prominent Mexican NGO, and the United Indigenous Totonaca and Nahuatl (UNITONA) of the Sierra Norte de Puebla.

The China Summer Work Camp is an opportunity for American, Chinese, Korean, and Japanese volunteers to teach English and environmental studies while building friendship and understanding among people from around the world. Work camp begins in Beijing with a few days of sightseeing and then participants travel to Hunan province in rural central

China where they will stay for three weeks teaching local children. There will be opportunities for visits to nearby towns, tours of local markets, hikes, and an overnight homestay with a city family. Volunteers must be at least 16 years old. A project fee is requested to cover all expenses except for personal incidentals, passport, visa, and vaccinations.

American Jewish World Service

45 West 36th Street, 11th floor, New York, NY 10018
Tel: (212) 792-2900
E-mail: volunteer@ajws.org
Website: www.ajws.org

American Jewish World Service (AJWS) is an international development organization dedicated to alleviating poverty, hunger, and disease among people of the global south regardless of race, religion or nationality. Through grants to grassroots organizations, volunteer service, advocacy, and education, AJWS fosters civil society, sustainable development, and human rights for all people, while promoting the values and responsibilities of global citizenship within the Jewish community. AJWS Volunteer Corps places professional Jewish women and men on volunteer assignments with local NGOs in the global south. Volunteers come from a variety of backgrounds and provide skills training, technical consultancy, and general support. VC volunteers range in age from young professionals to retirees, and share a passion for service and a commitment to social justice. AJWS World Partners Fellowship is awarded to recent Jewish college graduates and young professionals who wish to volunteer at an NGO, live independently in a country in the global south, and participate in a peer-learning community. Fellows learn about human rights in an international context, explore the Jewish values that motivate their work, and gain skills to prepare their entrance into careers dedicated to social justice. The fellowship has two main components: volunteer placement with an NGO and professional and leadership development.

Amigos de las Américas (AMIGOS) $ ⚕ ◫

5618 Star Lane, Houston, TX 77057
Tel: (800) 231-7796 *or* (713) 782-5290
Fax: (713) 782-9267
E-mail: info@amigoslink.org
Website: www.amigoslink.org

AMIGOS accepts volunteers 16 years and older who have studied two years of high school Spanish or the equivalent. Since 1965, AMIGOS has prepared enthusiastic, culturally sensitive volunteers to live with host families and work alongside community members. They help provide public health services, community development, and youth education. Projects are from four to eight weeks between June and August in Costa Rica, Dominican Republic, Honduras, Mexico, Nicaragua, Panama, Paraguay, and Uruguay. Volunteers work in teams of two or three. Former AMIGOS projects have included latrine and stove construction, environmental education, nutrition workshops, community garden organizing, health education, school renovations, rabies vaccinations, and youth group and sports league formation.

About 26 AMIGOS chapters across the US conduct training prior to departure and raise funds for the majority of the volunteers. College students and individuals who do not live in cities with chapters may apply as correspondent volunteers through the AMIGOS headquarters in Houston. The cost, which includes international airfare from Houston or Miami, housing with a family, food, project supplies, transportation, and short-term medical insurance, ranges from about $3,475 to $3,700. AMIGOS strongly encourages participant fundraising. Need-based financial assistance is available.

Amizade, Ltd.

PO Box 110107, Pittsburgh, PA 15232
Tel: (412) 441–6655
E-mail: volunteer@amizade.org
Website: www.amizade.org

Amizade is a nonprofit organization that encourages intercultural exploration and understanding through community-driven service-learning courses and volunteer programs. Participants cooperate with community partner organizations to complete sustainable, community-identified projects in education, health, and community development. Amizade participants have the opportunity to engage in a variety of volunteer positions while learning and exploring in a cross-cultural setting. Participants of all ages, backgrounds, and skill levels are welcome. Opportunities are currently available in Bolivia, Brazil, Ghana, Germany/Poland, Jamaica, Mexico, Northern Ireland, Tanzania, and the US (Washington DC, Greater Yellowstone Region, Montana, and Navajo Nation Arizona).

Amizade offers prescheduled programs for individuals and customized programs for groups. Customized individual volunteer placements ranging from two weeks to six months are currently available in Bolivia, Brazil, and Jamaica. The Amizade Global Service-Learning Consortium, a partnership with West Virginia University, offers service-learning courses and semesters that combine intercultural service and formal academic coursework for college credit (*www.globalservicelearning.org*).

The tax-deductible program fees start at $610 for a one-week domestic program and include room and board, ground transportation, cultural and educational activities, on-site staff, and a contribution to the host community.

Marvin Wachs, Volunteer, Amizade, 2001

When my wife and I retired in 2000 we wanted to travel, do something worthwhile for others, and live outside the US long enough to form a relationship with another country. We joined the construction brigades of four NGOs, testing the waters. Amizade was able to meet all of our requirements, especially by allowing us to be long-term volunteers for periods of our choosing. Following our initial "trial" run in 2001, we returned to Cochabamba, Bolivia, for six months in 2003, for three months in 2005, and we are returning shortly for three months in 2007. We have participated in nine work groups laying brick and tile as well as pouring concrete. Over the years we have participated in building both an orphanage and a rural school. We have done painting and renovation work at CEOLI, a center for the handicapped. Amizade's program in Bolivia is well organized. The in-country director and staff are native Bolivians with a strong commitment to their country and an intense desire to help volunteers have a good experience. We feel good about our experience with Amizade; they have earned our trust.

Bikes Not Bombs

(See listing under "US Voluntary Service Organizations")

Brethren Volunteer Service (BVS)

1451 Dundee Avenue, Elgin, IL 60120
Tel: (847) 742-5100 *or* (800) 323-8039
Fax: (847) 742-0278
E-mail: bvs_gb@brethren.org
Website: www.brethrenvolunteerservice.org

BVS is a program grounded in the Christian faith that brings a spiritual dimension to advocating justice, working for peace, serving basic human needs, and maintaining the integrity of creation. BVS places volunteers in Latin America (the Dominican Republic, Guatemala, Honduras, Nicaragua), Europe (Belgium, Bosnia-Herzegovina, Czech Republic, France, Germany, Ireland, Netherlands, Poland, Serbia-Yugoslavia, Slovakia, UK-Northern Ireland), Asia (Japan), and Africa (Nigeria). BVS also has one-year programs in the US. Positions abroad last two years and begin with a three-week orientation in the US. Volunteers are involved in a variety of community services: education, health care, office and construction work. Volunteers can also participate in ministry to children, youth, senior citizens, homeless, victims of domestic violence, prisoners, refugees, and persons with AIDS. Some positions require knowledge of a foreign language prior to orientation. Other requirements and special skills vary with assignments. Volunteers need not be Brethren or Christian but should be willing to examine the Christian faith. A college degree or equivalent life experience is required for overseas assignments. Travel expenses, room and board, medical coverage, and a monthly stipend of about $60 are provided. Some persons with physical disabilities can be accommodated, depending on the project.

Center for Environmental Education and Ecological Action (CEDUAM)

Centro de Educación Ambiental y Acción Ecológica A.C.
Col. Independencia No. 8, Tlaxco, Tlaxcala, Mexico, C.P. 90252
Tel: + (01 241) 496 135 *or* + (01 241) 420 7646
E-mail: info@ceduam.org
Website: http://ceduam.org

CEDUAM is a Mexican-run nonprofit organization of workers, farmers, and concerned citizens. For the past couple decades, CEDUAM has been building a popular ecological conscience in Tlaxco by offering six to seven free courses yearly on topics including organic horticulture and pest control, beekeeping, water and soil conservation, seed selection, traditional natural medicine, and fruit-tree maintenance. These in-depth courses are tools aimed at allowing local participants to achieve both ecological and economic sustainability. CEDUAM also hosts individuals and groups at its ecological recreation and education camp located in the Tlaxco foothills (2¹/₂ hours from Mexico City).

CEDUAM welcomes visitors to live and work at its camp for one week or (preferably) longer. The camp demonstrates how reforestation and drainage control can rehabilitate severely eroded landscapes. The site includes organic garden beds, a gray-water system, a traditional Temescal sweatlodge, and an extensive (mainly Spanish-language) library. CEDUAM offers rustic accommodations, kitchen/dining space, and lots of ways you can help out in its mountain setting. If you stay at the camp a modest fee is requested, which helps fund the courses.

Child Family Health International

995 Market Street #1104, San Francisco, CA 94103
Tel: (415) 957-9000 *or* (866) 345-4674
Fax: (415) 840-0486
E-mail: info@cfhi.org *or* students@cfhi.org
Website: www.cfhi.org

CFHI is a nonprofit organization providing health services to underserved communities worldwide by supporting local projects with essential medical supplies, volunteers, and funding. CFHI sends US medical, premedical, nursing, and other public health students to Bolivia, Ecuador, India, Mexico, and South Africa for training and service learning. Duties include hospital or clinical rotations and community education and outreach.

Participants should view their experience as an opportunity to develop cross-cultural and community health awareness, rather than to provide humanitarian aid. Programs vary in length from four to eight weeks. Spanish-language proficiency is useful for many of the placements, though language courses are often included in the program. Fees vary by program. Scholarships are available on a limited basis. Alumni services, including grants for health-care projects, are available.

Alumni, Child Family Health International, Andean Health in Quito Project, Ecuador

Andean Health provided an epiphany-like experience for me. Pursuing medicine is no longer the only goal. Now, I am challenged to find the underserved communities I will practice medicine within. Learning that there are not just illnesses, rather ill people, personalizes the mission of becoming a health-care provider.

Christian Peacemaker Teams (CPT) $ 🏴

PO Box 6508, Chicago, IL 60680-6508
Tel: (773) 277-0253
Fax: (773) 277-0291
E-mail: peacemakers@cpt.org
Website: www.cpt.org

CPT places teams of international volunteers in conflict settings as a violence-reduction presence. CPT is cross-denominational with strong roots grounded in the Quakers, Mennonites, and Church of the Brethren. CPT organizes long-term volunteers—the Christian Peacemaker Corps—to perform protective witness and accompaniment work in Colombia, Iraq, Palestine, and in Native Canadian communities in Ontario. Teams of four to twelve persons join the efforts of local peacemakers facing imminent violence. They accompany threatened individuals, report on human rights abuses, plan and execute nonviolent public responses to injustice, and train others in nonviolent direct action.

CPT emphasizes the Christian nature of its commitment to peace. All Christian Peacemaker Corps volunteers must attend training in nonviolent direct action, conflict de-escalation, and team building, either at CPT headquarters in Chicago or at regional sessions. Full-time corps members receive a small monthly stipend based on their living expenses and are expected to seek contributions to CPT in support of their work. CPT also maintains a reserve corps of trained volunteers who are on call for short periods of time. Corps volunteers and reservists must be at least 21 years old.

(Also listed under "Alternative Travel and Study Overseas")

Volunteer, Christian Peacemaker Team, Arizona Borderlands Delegation, 2005/2006

I really thought that the trip was mostly over when I left Tucson. Some processing, some increased interest in the issues, maybe some speaking. I was unprepared that the Borderlands issues would take on a life of their own within my life.... Thank you [to the delegation leader] for making these issues accessible and intelligible to me and the rest of our group.

Christians for Peace in El Salvador (CRISPAZ)

2 Lexington Street, East Boston, MA 02128
Tel: (617) 567-2900
Fax: (617) 249-0769
E-mail: info@crispaz.org
Website: www.crispaz.org

Founded in 1984, CRISPAZ is a faith-based organization dedicated to working with poor and marginalized communities in El Salvador. In building bridges of solidarity between communities in El Salvador and those in their home countries, CRISPAZ volunteers strive together for peace, justice, and human liberation. The long-term volunteer program is designed for individuals who wish to spend a minimum of one year living and working in a marginalized urban or rural community in El Salvador (with cultural immersion and orientation, allow 15 months). Long-term volunteers give of their time, skills, and interests as they work alongside Salvadorans in areas such as literacy, health care, pastoral work, community organization, education, agriculture, appropriate technology, and youth work.

The summer immersion program is designed to provide an intensive learning and service experience in a poor community in El Salvador. Interns live with Salvadorans and accompany them in their daily lives and work. Each intern will have the opportunity to contribute his or her skills to the communities. CRISPAZ provides volunteers with orientation, project placement, and support throughout the term of service.

(Also listed under "Alternative Travel and Study Overseas")

Community Agroecology Network (CAN) $ ✗✗

PO Box 7653, Santa Cruz, CA 95061-7653
Tel: (831) 459-3619
E-mail: cancoordinator@gmail.com
Website: www.communityagroecology.net

CAN's mission is to develop a network of rural communities and US consumers to support self-sufficiency and sustainable farming practices. To do this, CAN has worked primarily with coffee-growing communities in Central America. CAN believes that farmers who commit to working their land sustainably are best supported through a direct relationship with consumers, one that acknowledges and values the work involved with farming responsibly. CAN works with these communities in three ways:

1. COFFEE MARKETING:

Through a "fair trade direct" marketing system, coffee from the Coopepueblos Cooperative (southern Costa Rica) is sent directly to US and Canadian consumers. Since the coffee is processed, roasted, and packaged within the community, and mailed directly from the cooperative, every cent of the coffee purchase returns to the community. Profit is re-invested in farm projects, including the riparian reforesta-

tion, crop diversification, and the transition process to
organic production.

2. ACTION RESEARCH:

Farm-based research involves investigators and farmers,
with information generated from within and provided to
the community, including: in-depth studies of organizations
and social networks, and their relationship to community
and household livelihood with respect to development
goals; the role of cooperatives in alternative markets (direct,
organic, fair trade, etc.); interdisciplinary landscape-scale
analysis to better understand the social and environmental
causes of past and current changes in livelihoods and natural resources overtime; agroecological and ethnobotanical
studies of native shade trees and marketable species to
diversify coffee plantations and conserve native trees.

3. FIELD INTERNSHIPS*:

CAN field internships are rich learning experiences that
allow college students and graduates to match their unique
skills with particular projects. All interns live in homestays,
generally for 10-week periods. Previous projects have included a consumer education video on sustainability issues
in Coto Brus, establishing an agroecology demonstration
garden, interviews of ex-coffee farmers to document their
reasons for leaving, ornithological surveys of farms and
bioregion, experiments investigating the use of oil palm ash
for root knot nematode control in Coto Brus, and a green-
house project investigating vermicompost, broza (coffee
pulp) and compost tea (derived from coffee processing
"waste") as organic fertilizers for tomatoes and chilies
(high-value vegetable crops).

*FIELD INTERNSHIPS

• The Coto Brus (southern Costa Rica) internship, initiated
  in 1999, is the most established of CAN's three programs

Joey Smith, Intern, Community Agroecology Network, Agua Buena, Costa Rica, 2004

Spending three months in Agua Buena had tremendous impact on my life.

I began to realize that the most effective way to facilitate a connection between US consumers and Costa Rican farmers was through sharing stories I heard about the experiences of coffee cultivation, the effects of the coffee crisis, and the daily life in a small rural town. My host family, together with countless generous community members, welcomed me with open arms. The internship inspired me to bring these stories home. It also left me outraged at the amount of money actually received by most farmers, the ones who nurture the coffee plant 365 days a year. I was outraged at the pressures these farmers face to grow more and more coffee on their land: "Get big or get out." I was outraged at the environmental havoc this pressure wreaked on the most biologically diverse parts of the planet. I became more concerned about how much of current agriculture is beginning the long road to similarly destructive pressures. Yet, I found hope in the husband and wife I was living with who were constantly finding ways to apply their ethics to their land. Whether through the pig-poop-powered stove, nitrogen-fixing shade trees planted among the coffee, strategically planted grass to prevent erosion during almost daily downpours, or current experiments with diversified vegetable crops, they are putting the word "sustainable" in action. They are able to do this directly because of the higher price received from fair-trade direct coffee sales.

It is my hope that CAN and its model of education, research, and direct marketing can spread to other agricultural crops. To me, increasing and deepening the connection between all parts of the food system is one of the surest ways to further a culture of respect that will be essential to making trade truly fair.

in Central America. This program accepts motivated interns who can work collaboratively and independently. Spanish language skills are preferred, but not required. Interns work on various projects through the Coope-pueblos Cooperative.

• The Matagalpa, Nicaragua, program accepts motivated interns with intermediate to high-level Spanish skills, who have a strong desire to work with small coffee coop-eratives in the mountains of northern Nicaragua. In addition to an increased return for their organic coffee through CAN, these communities are working on a burgeoning agro-ecotourism program. This internship is co-facilitated with CECOCAFEN, a larger cooperative representing 1,900 small-scale coffee farmers in the north of Nicaragua.

• The Tacuba, El Salvador, program is open to independ-ently motivated interns with high proficiency in written and spoken Spanish. Previous experience abroad is pre-ferred. Interns work with ASINDEC (Advising and Interdisciplinary Research on Local Development and Conservation), a nonprofit, apolitical organization formed by environment and rural development researchers.

Concern America $ ✂

2015 North Broadway, Santa Ana, CA 92706
Mailing address: PO Box 1790, Santa Ana, CA 92702
Tel: (714) 953-8575 *or* (800) 266-2376
Fax: (714) 953-1242
E-mail: concamerinc@earthlink.net
Website: www.concernamerica.org

Concern America is an international development and refugee aid organization whose main objective is to provide training, technical assistance, and material support to community-based programs in refugee camps and in the global south. Concern America volunteers serve for at least two years and are professionals such as physicians, nurses, nutritionists, community organizers, and specialists in agriculture, appropriate technology, public health, and sanitation. The focus of the work is on training local people to carry on programs that include healthcare education, developing nutrition and sanitation projects, organizing community development and income-generating projects, and conducting literacy campaigns. Concern America volunteers currently serve in Bolivia, Colombia, El Salvador, Honduras, Guatemala, Mexico, and Mozambique. Volunteers must be at least 21 years old and fluent in Spanish if serving in Latin America. Concern America provides transportation, room and board, health insurance, a small stipend, and a repatriation allowance.

Cross-Cultural Solutions (CCS)

2 Clinton Place, New Rochelle, NY 10801
Tel: (800) 380–4777 *or* (914) 632–0022
Fax: (914) 632–8494
E-mail: info@crossculturalsolutions.org
Website: www.crossculturalsolutions.org

Founded in 1995, CCS is an international not-for-profit organization with no political or religious affiliations. As a recognized leader in the field of international volunteering, CCS enables volunteers to make meaningful contributions to the community by working side by side with local people, while gaining a new perspective and insight into the culture and themselves. CCS has a worldwide staff of over 200 people with administrative offices located in the US, UK, and Canada. Volunteers work with carefully selected partner programs on community-led initiatives including orphanages and childcare centers, schools, health clinics and hospitals, homes for the elderly, centers for people with disabilities, and other community organizations. Programs are one to twelve weeks long with programs in Brazil, China, Costa Rica, Ghana, Guatemala, India, Morocco, Peru, Russia, South Africa, Tanzania, and Thailand. The two-week program fee starts at $2,489 and is tax deductible in the US.

Helen Barr, Volunteer, Cross-Cultural Solutions

As a result of [CCS's] care in matching volunteer skills, interests, and hopes to programs, my volunteer time in Thailand and Peru exceeded expectations. I spent no longer than six weeks in each place, but I felt the time I spent with street children in Bangkok and in Lima mattered in their day-to-day experiences. Alongside such disadvantage, learning about its causes and helping to make daily life for those children creative, fun, and, most of all, safe, I felt my presence did matter. Days matter.

It's now nearly a year since my first program in Thailand. Not a day goes by when I do not think of the people I worked with. The work does not stop once you come home; volunteering does not stop once the TV screen hovers into view again—by stepping into the space behind, you've crossed that all-important barrier.

Doctors for Global Health (DGH)

PO Box 1761, Decatur, GA 30031
Tel/Fax: (404) 377-3566
E-mail: volunteer@dghonline.org
Website: www.dghonline.org

DGH is a private nonprofit organization promoting health and human rights with those who have no voice. Founded in 1995, DGH strives to promote health, education, social justice, and human rights by funding and carrying out projects in cooperation with local nonprofit and nongovernmental partner organizations in interested communities. With an emphasis on community-oriented primary care, liberation medicine, and volunteerism, DGH works with communities in El Salvador, Nicaragua, Mexico, Guatemala, Argentina, Uganda, and the US. Various volunteer opportunities are available, depending on the volunteer's skills and the needs and desires of the local community. Most volunteer activities involve health care, education, and public health activities. DGH prefers long-term volunteers, but does occasionally accept volunteers for minimum stays of one to two months. Volunteers should expect to pay for their own travel expenses, food, and lodging.

Wendy Hobson, MD, Volunteer, Doctors for Global Health, El Salvador

I have spent most of my time working on the Improving Women's Reproductive Health and Human Rights in Southeastern Morazán campaign. Steve and Irma worked out the details of the project so that when I arrived we were practically ready to begin. In a two-day training session we taught MDM health promoters, health promoters from the Ministry of Health, and local midwives basic information about female anatomy, STDs, gynecological cancers, and human rights. This training prepared participants to give a brief talk at the beginning of each of our scheduled community visits. During these two days, I grasped what the reality is for many of these women: They have to live in a society where women are not valued nearly as much as men. The machismo begins at birth—a midwife receives a considerably higher fee for delivering a baby boy than a baby girl. Many of the women are not permitted to leave their homes to go to the clinic, while the men may roam the streets at night and have relations with different women. One notes the discrepancy even in the children's play: There always seem to be little boys playing soccer in the street while the little girls are at home helping their mothers in the kitchen or watching their smaller brothers and sisters.

After writing and revising the 34-page-long project, we jumped right into the first phase of community visits. The project covers a two-year time span (I was able to participate only in the first phase, but I would love to return for the later phases). Each day began with the construction of the exam rooms, using sheets and hammocks as walls. Following that the health promoters gave an interactive lecture on human rights, breast and cervical cancer, the vaginal exam, and STDs. Then we took data and finally performed the examinations. Steve looked at samples for trichomonas [a parasite that causes a common STD], candidiasis [yeast infection], and bacterial vaginosis [vaginal infection] in our ambulatory lab, and we sent other samples to the Department of Microbiology at the National University of El Salvador for further analysis. All of the activity made for a very full day, everyday.

The work was always a challenge—providing a mobile gynecology clinic in rural El Salvador is not an easy task—and each community offered a different surprise in coordinating efforts. In Babylonia we had to carry the tables and equipment for a 15-minute walk down an impassable road, and a few days later, back up again. The two days of the actual project at least 11 community members helped throughout the day. The community's participation is essential in these projects.

Doctors Without Borders-USA, Inc.

Médecins Sans Frontières (MSF)
333 7th Avenue, 2nd Floor, New York, NY 10001-5004
Tel: (212) 679-6800 or (888) 392-0392
Fax: (212) 679-7016
E-mail: doctors@newyork.msf.org
Website: www.doctorswithoutborders.org

Doctors Without Borders/Médecins Sans Frontières (MSF) is an independent international medical humanitarian organization that delivers emergency aid to people affected by armed conflict, epidemics, natural or man-made disasters, or lacking health care in more than 70 countries. Each year, MSF doctors, nurses, logisticians, water-and-sanitation experts, administrators, and other medical and nonmedical professionals depart on more than 4,700 aid assignments. They work alongside more than 25,800 locally hired staff to provide medical care. MSF's decision to intervene in any country or crisis is based solely on an independent assessment of people's needs—not on political, economic, or religious interests. MSF does not take sides or intervene according to the demands of governments or warring parties. Solid professional experience is essential in the field. All medical professionals must have a valid license to practice and two years of postgraduate professional work experience. The minimum volunteer commitment is six months; a year's commitment is more typical. A good working knowledge of a foreign language is highly valued. Familiarity with tropical medicine is an asset.

Fellowship of Reconciliation (FOR)
Task Force on Latin America and the Caribbean
Colombia Peace Presence
2017 Mission Street #200, San Francisco, CA 94110
Tel: (415) 495-6334
Fax: (415) 495-5628
E-mail: forcolombia@igc.org
Website: www.forcolombia.org

The FOR Colombia Peace Presence provides protective human rights accompaniment to nonviolent grassroots communities and groups in Colombia working for justice and peace, including the Peace Community of San José de Apartadó, where FOR maintains a permanent team. FOR also has a team in Bogotá that visits other partner groups around the country to increase their visibility, support, and security. Teamwork includes gathering information, writing reports, meeting with officials, organizing visits by delegations, and office/home maintenance. Volunteers must be 23 years old, proficient in Spanish and English, committed to values of nonviolence, and able to commit for one year. Qualified applicants participate in training in the US and Colombia, and are expected to share their experiences on return.

Dan Malakoff, Volunteer, Fellowship of Reconciliation, 2005/2006

As a teenager, I volunteered in Nicaragua and Cuba, where I met people who suffered because of US foreign policy: the US-sponsored civil war against the popular Sandinista government in the 1980s Nicaragua and the trade embargo against Cuba. Today, the US government—*my* government—fuels a civil war in another Latin American country: Colombia. After college, when I learned that the Fellowship of Reconciliation was on the ground there, helping shield civilians from this war, I signed up.

On FOR's behalf, I spent a year in the Peace Community of San José de Apartadó, a collection of villages and hamlets that, for having adopted a radical pacifist stance against the war and all its armed participants, endures grave persecution. The *campesinos* that formed the Peace Community are small-scale chocolate bean and banana farmers who want only to keep their lands. Today, the community claims 1500 members; in its 10-year history, over 150 have been murdered. The leftist guerrilla kills anyone it suspects— often on little more than rumor—of collaborating with the government. The US-backed Colombian army, working with rightist paramilitaries, threatens with unjust arrests, abuses, selectively assassinates, and massacres in a campaign to empty the countryside and isolate the guerrillas. Every single person in the Peace Community risks these dangers for a way of life. I couldn't think of anyone more deserving of support or anywhere I would rather live and volunteer.

Two of us, as a "field" team, worked as *acompañantes*, accompaniers. (FOR maintains a second accompaniment team in Colombia's capital, Bogotá.) It worked like this: Sunday in San José is market day, when *campesinos* on far-away farms come to town to play cards or soccer, gossip, buy sugar and rice. On one such Sunday, combat between the army and the guerrillas flared between town and an outlying settlement called Arenas Altas, or High Sands. After the gunfire quieted, the community organized a caravan. We were asked to go with these stranded *campesinos*, too scared of being caught in the crossfire or targeted in reprisal to return without accompaniment; our presence would help deter any aggression. We made the two-hour journey, past the soldiers and checkpoints, the guerrillas moving or lying in wait nearby, so that these people could safely return to their homes.

We also acted as a bridge to the outside world. As human rights observers, we collected and disseminated the facts so that rights violators couldn't hide behind the "fog of war." International attention, in turn, curbed future attacks. One day, we hope to end US military involvement in Colombia.

On most days—and this was what I most loved—we went with the workers into their fields, shared stories over dinners of rice and beans, and, from the stoop, listened to nocturnal frogs and cicadas and the playing children's laughter. On these days, I got a taste of what peace meant to this community and how fulfilled I felt to contribute to that peace.

Foundation for Sustainable Development (FSD)

870 Market Street, Suite 321, San Francisco, CA 94102
Tel/Fax: (415) 283-4873
E-mail: info@fsdinternational.org
Website: www.fsdinternational.org

Since 1995, FSD has provided technical training, funding, and human resources to nearly 200 nongovernmental and grassroots organizations throughout Latin America, East Africa, and India. FSD relies on volunteers and interns to support these organizations and facilitate project work that makes efficient use of grant funds. FSD's nonprofit model gives 100 percent of grants received to the communities they serve. The money is distributed via program participants, who apply for project funding after establishing a viable work plan.

FSD believes that sustainable development is a dynamic process that must interweave pragmatism with cultural awareness. While working to support economic, social, and educational programs, FSD recognizes that what lies at the heart of effective solutions are the local communities. Understanding their beliefs, values, and worldviews is essential to designing appropriate projects.

FSD trains volunteers and interns by immersing them in the community to learn about local needs, values, and solutions. Once this is achieved, participants are trained and given the opportunity to comprehensively create, fund, and implement sustainable projects in collaboration with their host organization and FSD's in-country support staff. Participants gain valuable development experience and training while making relationships that change their lives.

Program costs vary. Credit and scholarships may be available.

Kate Vyborny, Volunteer, Foundation for Sustainable Development

At 11 p.m. the meeting is not even close to over. Two men and a woman in traditional Salasca dress shout at the same time, arguing in Quechua about how the profits from a cheese-making project will be divided. Several women in the meeting breastfeed their babies as they listen; children play outside, some getting tired and deciding to walk home alone through the dark fields. The president of the community occasionally breaks in and translates into Spanish for me....

A group of traditional artisans asked for help exporting their weavings, and I looked for Fair Trade suppliers; then I helped them apply to sell their work to these organizations. I had the privilege of serving two indigenous communities in rural Ecuador, and experiencing the challenges of community development firsthand. It was part of my job to attend meetings like this, hear what the people here hope for to improve their lives, and try to help make it happen.

Fourth World Movement/USA

Maryland Center: 7600 Willow Hill Drive, Landover, MD 20785-4658
Tel: (301) 336-9489
Fax: (301) 336-0092
Washington, DC Office: 734 15th Street NW, #525, Washington, DC 20005
Tel: (202) 393-2822
Fax: (202) 393-2443
E-mail: nationalcenter@4thworldmovement.org
Website: www.4thworldmovement.org

Fourth World Movement's work has three priorities: learning
from the most disadvantaged families, understanding how they
become trapped in persistent poverty, and planning and developing projects with them. Accepted applicants first do a two- to
three-month internship (offered spring, summer, and fall), living and working with full-time Volunteer Corps members at
the New York, New Orleans, Appalachian, or Washington, DC,
area centers. Interns receive free housing and transportation.
They learn about Fourth World Movement and its approach to
persistent poverty through their project work and through
videos, readings, and discussion. Interns are expected to be flexible and available to help a given team with its current projects,
not all of which are grassroots. At the end of the internship,
interns discuss with their supervisors whether they will go on
to join the Volunteer Corps for a minimum two-year commitment. This begins in North America; there is no guarantee of
an assignment overseas. Placement is made according to both
an intern's interests and Fourth World Movement's needs.
There are currently teams in 30 countries and six continents.

(Also listed under "Alternative Travel and Study Overseas")

Frontiers Foundation/Operation Beaver

419 Coxwell Avenue, Toronto, Ontario M4L-3B9, Canada
Tel: (416) 690-3930
Fax: (416) 690-3934
E-mail: frontiersfoundation@on.aibn.com
Website: www.frontiersfoundation.ca

Frontiers Foundation is a community-development service organization that works in partnership with communities in low-income rural areas across northern Canada. These locally initiated projects build and improve housing, conduct training programs, and organize educational and recreational activities in the global south. Volunteers must be 18 years of age or older and available for a minimum of 12 weeks. Skills in carpentry, electrical work, and plumbing are preferred for construction projects. Previous social service and experience with children are preferred for recreation and education projects. Accommodations, food, and travel inside Canada are provided.

Global Routes

1 Short Street, Northampton, MA 01060
Tel: (413) 585-8895
Fax: (413) 585-8810
E-mail: mail@globalroutes.org
Website: www.globalroutes.org

Global Routes, a tax-exempt nonprofit, is a nongovernmental, nonsectarian organization that designs experiential community service projects and teaching internships for high school and college-aged students. By living and working with people in rural communities throughout the world, program participants gain a better sense of themselves, the world, and their place in it. High school programs are three, four, and five weeks long in the summer. Destinations include Belize, China, Costa Rica, Ecuador, Dominican Republic, France, Ghana, India, Kenya, Mexico, Nepal, Peru, and Thailand.

The college-level teaching internship is eight to twelve weeks long and offered in the summer, fall, winter, and spring. Teaching internships currently exist in Costa Rica, Ecuador, Ghana, India, Kenya, and Thailand. All Global Routes programs have trained staff members on-site. Participants pay program fees and airfare.

Global Vision International (GVI)

North America: 252 Newbury Street, No. 4, Boston, MA 02116 USA
Tel: (888) 653-6028
E-mail: info@gviusa.com
Website: www.gviusa.com
United Kingdom: 3 High Street, St. Albans, Herts, AL3 4ED, UK
Tel: + (44) 870 608 8898
E-mail: info@gvi.co.uk
Website: www.gvi.co.uk

Over 150 critical conservation and humanitarian projects in over 30 countries rely on GVI for volunteers, promotion, and direct funding. GVI works locally with its partners to promote sustainable development through environmental research, conservation, and education. Because GVI runs long-term projects, there is opportunity to volunteer all year-round. Project lengths vary from a week to a year in duration.

GVI sees the importance of offering opportunities for all, whether retired, taking a career break, or on a gap year before or after university. There is an application process with support from local offices. Training is supplied on all projects to successful applicants who demonstrate interest and awareness of cultural sensitivities. In 2006 GVI placed over 2,000 volunteers, from 29 countries, 18 to 78 years of age. The cost starts from £900 (€1300), depending on the length and type (expedition, project, or courses) of the trip, and include food, accommodation, and a significant financial donation to the project. In 2006, 78 percent of volunteer contributions were spent directly in field. GVI provides resources including field packs, training manuals, kit lists, an online forum to meet other volunteers, partner offers on flights, insurance, guidebooks, and clothing. Additionally, GVI provides overseas in-country coordinators, a 24-hour manned phone line, airport pickup and drop off, and in-country orientation. With unparalleled in-country support, GVI volunteers benefit from exceptional training and a careers abroad job placement scheme. All 10-week expedition members are eligible for an internship, to stay on for a further research phase free of charge. For details on careers with GVI, including paid fieldwork roles, visit www.careersabroad.co.uk. GVI commits to safe, responsible travel experiences, exceptional training, career development opportunities, and the chance to make a real difference on real projects, set up by local people, with local aims.

> **Nicholas Faherty, Expedition Member, Global Vision International, Mexico, 2007**
>
> I have now participated in two different Global Vision International expeditions and see that they truly care for the communities they work in as well as the travelers who desire to do more than the normal tourist experience.

Global Volunteer Network (GVN)

PO Box 30-968, Lower Hutt, New Zealand
Tel: + (644) 569-9080
Fax: + (644) 569-9081
E-mail: info@volunteer.org.nz
Website: www.volunteer.org.nz

GVN supports local community organizations through the placement of international volunteers. Opportunities are currently available in Alaska (US), China, Ecuador, El Salvador, Ghana, Nepal, New Zealand, Romania, Russia, Thailand, Uganda, and Vietnam. Volunteers can be involved in areas such as teaching English, environmental work, animal welfare, and health education. Program placements range from two weeks to a year, and are available to those aged 18 and up. While relevant experience enables volunteers to further enhance GVN programs, most placements do not require special skills. People with physical disabilities are considered on a case-by-case basis. The application fee is $297, followed by monthly program fees ranging from $250 to $700, which cover the volunteer's food, housing, and most other in-country expenses.

Global Volunteers (GV)

375 East Little Canada Road, St. Paul, MN 55117-1627
Tel: (800) 487-1074 *or* (651) 407-6100
Fax: (651) 482-0915
E-mail: email@globalvolunteers.org
Website: www.globalvolunteers.org

Global Volunteers, founded in 1984, forms teams of volunteers who live in host communities and work with local people on development projects selected by local leadership. The projects may involve teaching conversational English; constructing and renovating schools and clinics; providing health care, child care, business planning; or assisting in other local activities. Opportunities are available in Africa, Asia, Australia, the Pacific Islands, Europe, Latin America, the Caribbean, and the US. Volunteers are of all ages and come from all backgrounds and occupations, including teachers, carpenters, homemakers, physicians, and artists. No special skills or languages are required. Tax-deductible program fees range from $795 to $2,695 and include costs of training, ground transportation, lodging, project materials, all meals, and an experienced team leader. The organization also offers child-sponsorship programs in China, India, Ecuador, Tanzania, and Romania.

Nikki Hauspurg, Volunteer, Global Volunteers, Construction Project, Costa Rica

In June 2004 I found myself sandwiched into a middle seat on United Flight 914 departing from San Jose, Costa Rica, destined for Dulles International Airport, exhausted, yet exhilarated. I wondered how I appeared to my fellow passengers, clutching a glutted backpack of Fair Trade coffee, dirty and disheveled, and feeling as though my skin was three layers thicker than when I had first arrived weeks earlier. I carried with me the constant exposure to sun, dust, and mosquito repellent. As I adjusted my seat, careful not to hit my bandaged knee on the tray table, I began to reminisce about my Global Volunteers experience. I had been part of a team whose goal was to assist in the creation of a community center for the impoverished populace of Canitas, Costa Rica.

I had been nervous the first day as I met my teammates, realizing that as a high school senior at 5'3" and 100 pounds I was not only the youngest team member, but also the smallest in stature. As the team leader described the mission of our American team —an endeavor that aimed at laboring with, and not merely for, the residents of Canitas—I tried to imagine how I could make a substantial contribution to this international effort. While initially intimidated, at the conclusion of my first day at our workplace—a dusty construction site within a pastoral village of Costa Rica—I had already begun to witness different ways in which I could contribute to our group's mission.

Although the youngest team member, I realized I was the most proficient in Spanish, and thus became vital to the team dynamic in establishing connections between the American and Costa Rican workers. In translating jokes, asking for tools, and working with female villagers to cook tamales for lunch, I came to appreciate my understanding of the native language. It facilitated new friendships and supplemented my team in the workplace. Furthermore, I began to value my small frame, for I discovered that in working with a group of sturdy, male Cost Ricans to construct the septic system for the community center, my size became an asset in maneuvering into narrow pits in order to connect PVC pipes and retrieve fallen tools. During this service opportunity I also realized that physical labor does not merely require physical strength. On one occasion, I was assigned the task of using a pick-axe to penetrate a 6-inch cinder block wall in order to connect the PVC from the outside septic system to the inside fixture. The tenacious Costa Rican locals made the task look easy, piercing through the wall with several blows that resulted in a rough opening. However, the PVC would not fit. By using a chisel and hammer I found I could direct my strength effectively, and refine the rough opening into a near-symmetrical hole that was just wide enough for the PVC pipe to be connected, with a minimal amount of patchwork.

My experiences in Canitas were not solely based upon grunt work, however. Through this volunteer opportunity, I learned that in order to spur progress, and effectively contribute to a community on a global scale, one must take personal risks. One must be immersed in a new culture. While I learned lessons of self-worth and the value of a strong work ethic, perhaps most significantly, I came away with an appreciation of an Ethiopian proverb I once came across: "When spider webs unite, they can tie up a lion." While my personal skills may have contributed to the team dynamic, it was the union of each teammate's contributions that made our volunteer efforts a success. Beyond anything I could have contributed to Canitas, I gained the immeasurable gift of awareness: I realized the vastness of the world around me, and began to consider how I could contribute on a larger scale.

As I sat in my plane seat, I reflected on one last memory: I had tripped on an uneven gravel road while carrying construction materials to the worksite, and in doing so split open my knee. Both my American and Costa Rican teammates rushed to my side to lift me up and help me to a neighbor's home. As I apologized (awkwardly, bilingually) and thanked them, they orchestrated a small-scale surgery on a kitchen table. As they removed as much gravel as was possible and bandaged my bleeding knee, I realized how much I would miss the optimistic collectivism I had experienced in Canitas.

It has been three months since I left Costa Rica, but as I touch the tiny fragments of gravel that remain imbedded in my knee, I know I will always have a tangible reminder of this trip, which solidified my goal of pursuing a career in foreign service.

Hands for Help Nepal

Post Box No. 9012, Nawasngam Marga-10, Kathmandu Metropolitan
    City—29 Kathmandu, Nepal
Tel: + (977) 1-4362648
Fax: + (977) 1-4700432
E-mail: info@handsforhelp.com
Website: www.handsforhelp.com

Hands for Help Nepal is a nonprofit, nongovernmental organization that sends volunteers to various projects in Nepal. Currently Hands for Help Nepal provides volunteer opportunities that including teaching in schools, assisting in orphanages and community health clinics, teaching English in a Buddhist monastery, school construction and renovation, and teaching environmental awareness. Programs last from one to five months. Volunteers must be at least 17 years old. The cost is $500 for the first month and $150 for each additional month.

Incarnate Word Missionaries (IWM)

4503 Broadway, San Antonio, TX 78209-6297
Tel: (210) 828-2224, ext. 228
Fax: (210) 828-9741
E-mail: iwmissionaries@amormeus.org
Website: www.amormeus.org

IWM seeks a new economic, social, and political order promoting justice and solidarity. Missionaries work with homeless women and children and indigenous peoples performing services that may include human rights work, health care, clinic/hospice ministry, and pastoral ministry. Missionaries serve in the US, Guatemala, Mexico, Peru, and throughout Africa.

IWM missionaries must be at least 21 years old, in good physical and mental health, single or married without dependents, willing to commit to one year in their own country or two to three years in a country other than their own, willing to live a simple lifestyle, open to working with a preferential option for the poor, and of the Christian faith (some sites require that one be Catholic). Those who wish to serve in Latin America must have some degree of fluency in the Spanish language.

The missionary pays the cost of transportation to the orientation site, language school, and vacation travel and emergency leave, as well as any costs incurred for preexisting medical conditions. All other costs are paid by IWM.

InterConnection
(Their web–savvy work in support of worldwide NGOs is done without leaving home. See the listing under "US Voluntary Service Organizations")

International Society for Ecology and Culture (ISEC)
PO Box 9475, Berkeley, CA 94709
Tel: (510) 548–4915
Fax: (510) 548–4916
E–mail: infousa@isec.org.uk
Website: www.isec.org.uk or
     http://www.isec.org.uk/pages/learningfromladakh.html

ISEC is concerned with raising awareness about the root causes of today's social, environmental, and economic crises. In challenging economic globalization and conventional notions of "progress," ISEC promotes localization, thereby helping to strengthen community and restore the environment. ISEC produces books, videos, and other educational material and promotes grassroots and policy-level strategies for ecological and community renewal.

ISEC's Learning from Ladakh (formerly The Farm Project) program arranges one-month farm stays during July and August. Participants live and work with Ladakhi families in northern India and are exposed to both the strengths of Ladakhi traditional culture and the forces threatening to undermine it. The cost is $600, which includes room and board on the farm. Volunteers are expected to cover their own travel expenses. Ladakh is located at extremely high altitudes and requires a great deal of manual labor, so volunteers should be able to work under these conditions.

Interplast

857 Maude Avenue, Mountain View, CA 94043
Tel: (888) 467-5278 *or* (650) 962-0123
Fax: (650) 962-1619
E-mail: volunteers@interplast.org *or* info@interplast.org
Website: www.interplast.org

Interplast is a nonprofit organization partnering with physicians in countries of the global south to provide free reconstructive plastic surgery for needy children and adults. Interplast coordinates support and advanced training for local surgeons and manages volunteer service programs to care for more than 3,000 impoverished patients every year. Interplast's programs provide surgeries for patients with congenital deformities (cleft lip, cleft palate) or those with severe burns, hand injuries, or other crippling injuries. Interplast's scope of services includes supporting surgeons in countries of the global south to manage their own outreach programs, sending volunteer medical teams overseas to perform the needed surgeries and assist in skills transfer, and conducting workshops that provide advanced training in specialized skills for host country medical professionals.

Working at more than 25 different sites in over 12 countries in Africa, Central and South America, and South and Southeast Asia, Interplast has provided almost 57,000 surgeries since 1969. Interplast has six surgical outreach centers in: Bangladesh, Ecuador, Nepal, Peru (two), and Zambia. Plastic surgeons, pediatricians, anesthesiologists, operating room nurses, and recovery room nurses are needed in a volunteer capacity. Each team also requires a secretary/translator who provides general patient, family, and team support and performs clerical work.

Jesuit Volunteer Corps (JVC) $ 🏠

PO Box 3756, Washington, DC 20027-0256
Website: www.jesuitvolunteers.org

Each year JVC offers about 500 men and women the opportunity to work full time for justice and peace by serving the poor directly and working for structural change. The challenge to Jesuit Volunteers (JVs) is to integrate Christian faith by working and living among the poor, living modestly in a cooperative household with other JVs, and examining the causes of social injustice. JVs serve as teachers, counselors, nurses, social workers, community organizers, and lawyers, and work with the homeless, physically and mentally ill, elderly, children, refugees, prisoners, and migrant workers. JVs serve in Belize, Bolivia, Chile, Haiti, the Marshall Islands, Micronesia, Nepal, Nicaragua, Peru, South Africa, Tanzania, and the US.

JVC welcomes women and men from diverse backgrounds. Applicants must have a Christian motivation, be 21 or older, have a college degree or applicable work experience, and be without dependents. There is a particular need for applicants competent in Spanish.

Domestic placements are for one year and begin in August. International placements require a two-year commitment and also begin in August. JVC provides room and board, health insurance, a small personal stipend, local support teams, workshops and retreats during the year, transportation home at the end of the term of service, and an active alumni association. See the JVC website for regional contact information.

Joint Assistance Center, Inc. (JAC)   ◩

PO Box 6082, San Pablo, CA 94806-0082
Tel: (510) 237-8331
Fax: (510) 217-6671
E-mail: jacusa@juno.com
Website: www.jacusa.org

JAC is a nongovernmental voluntary organization headquartered in Haryana State in the outskirts of Delhi, India. It coordinates conferences and training in various parts of India on disaster preparedness and works in liaison with groups, individuals, and small grassroots projects throughout the country. JAC focuses on community, welfare, health, education, youth development, and agricultural training. It welcomes volunteers from around the world to participate in the work of its partner organizations. Short-term projects (minimum one month) can involve sanitation, construction, agriculture, the environment, public health, or literacy. Long-term projects (three months or more) are similar to the short-term ones but allow for greater depth.

JAC programs run year-round. Arrangements must be made at least 30 days in advance of the volunteer's arrival in India. Volunteers participate in an orientation program in New Delhi before departing for their assigned village. In New Delhi volunteers stay at a JAC-maintained dormitory; accommodations at work camps are in homes, schools, or other public buildings. The registration fee is $50, and the cost for one month is $230. For a long-term placement, the fee is $550 for the first three months and $125 for each month thereafter. Airfare is not included. JAC also coordinates volunteer programs with organizations in Bangladesh, Nepal, and South Korea.

Maryknoll Lay Missioners

Maryknoll Mission Association of the Faithful, Inc.
PO Box 307, Maryknoll, NY 10545-0307
Tel: (800) 818-5276 ext. 114 or 122
Fax: (914) 762-7031
E-mail: kwright@mklm.org
Website: http://laymissioners.maryknoll.org

Maryknoll Mission Association of the Faithful, popularly known as Maryknoll Lay Missioners, is part of the Maryknoll mission family. Maryknoll Lay Missioners is a Catholic organization inspired by the mission of Jesus to live and work with poor communities in Africa, Asia, and the Americas, responding to basic needs and helping to create a more just and compassionate world. Missioners come from a wide range of professional and educational backgrounds and may serve in the fields of health (including direct service to people with AIDS), education, community organizing, grassroots economic development, and formation of faith communities. Mission sites are located in Brazil, Bolivia, Cambodia, Chile, East Timor, El Salvador, Kenya, Mexico, Nepal, Panama, Peru, Tanzania, Thailand, Venezuela, Vietnam, Zimbabwe, and on the US–Mexico border.

Mennonite Central Committee (MCC)

PO Box 500, Akron, PA 17501–0500
Tel: (717) 859–1151
Fax: (717) 859–2171
E-mail: mailbox@mcc.org
Website: www.mcc.org

MCC is the cooperative relief, service, and peace agency of the Mennonite and Brethren in Christ churches in North America. Currently just over 1,200 people serve in agriculture, health, education, social services, and community development fields in 55 countries, including the US and Canada. Qualifications depend on assignment. Transportation, living expenses, and a small stipend are provided. MCC asks that volunteers be Christian, actively involved in a church congregation, and in agreement with MCC's nonviolent principles. Placements are for three years overseas or two years in North America.

Middle East Children's Alliance (MECA)
(See listing under "Alternative Travel and Study Overseas")

MondoChallenge

Malsor House, Gayton Road, Milton Malsor, Northampton NN7 3AB,
    United Kingdom
Tel: + (44 160) 485–8225
Fax: + (44 160) 485–9323
E-mail: info@mondochallenge.org
Website: www.mondochallenge.org

MondoChallenge is a mid-sized NGO based in England that matches motivated volunteers (with particular emphasis in teaching or business) with short-term community-generated projects in Chile, Ecuador, Tanzania, Kenya, Gambia, Senegal, India, Nepal, Sri Lanka, and Romania. The volunteer placement ranges from one to six months and is ideal for people of various ages seeking to make a positive impact (and who are ready to be similarly impacted). Potential volunteers over 18 years old need only have an interest in education to work on projects, including HIV/AIDS awareness and support for affected communities. Those interested in business development projects are asked to have four years' relevant experience. The average three-month placement currently costs volunteers the equivalent of $1950.

Network in Solidarity with the People of Guatemala (NISGUA)

$ 🕸

Guatemala Accompaniment Project (GAP)
1830 Connecticut Avenue NW, Washington, DC 20009
Tel: (202) 265-8713
Fax: (202) 223-8221
E-mail: gap@nisgua.org
Website: www.nisgua.org

NISGUA's Guatemala Accompaniment Project creates a nonviolent response to the threats, harassment, and violence faced by survivors of Guatemala's 36-yearlong civil war and by grassroots organizations working for justice and human rights. Through GAP, volunteers live alongside threatened individuals and communities in an effort to deter human rights violations. These volunteers, known as accompaniers, monitor the situation and alert the international community to abuses. The accompaniers' presence provides a measure of security and creates space for Guatemalan communities and organizations working to defend their rights. Volunteers commit to a minimum of six months of service and are at least 21 years old. Potential accompaniers should have: an understanding of the history of Central America–US relationships, and the current situation in Guatemala; an understanding of accompaniment and nonviolence, and a willingness to continue developing that understanding; previous experience in Latin America (strongly preferred); a proficiency in Spanish or the ability to develop it with six weeks of study; the ability to document and analyze; cultural sensitivity; excellent judgment skills; physical stamina and good health; awareness of security issues and willingness to work in a situation that might involve some risk; and US residency, or a strong connection to a community in the US. Accompaniers must also successfully complete the GAP training.

Estimated expenses for the volunteer are from $520 to $2,270. NISGUA provides training on grassroots fundraising techniques. Accompaniers in the field receive a stipend and other program-related costs are covered. GAP can sometimes accommodate people with physical disabilities.

Nicaragua Network

1247 E Street SE, Washington, DC 20003
Tel: (202) 544-9355
Fax: (202) 544-9359
E-mail: nicanet@afgj.org
Website: www.nicanet.org

For a quarter of a century the Nicaragua Network has been a leading organization in the US committed to social and economic justice for Nicaragua and Latin America, based upon respect for sovereignty and self-determination. The Network advocates for sound US foreign policies that respect human rights and international law. The Nicaragua Network provides information and organizing tools to a network of 200 solidarity, sister-city, and peace and justice committees across the US.

Publications include the *Nicaragua Network Hotline*, the *Nicaragua News Service*, the *Nicaragua Monitor*, and occasional monographs. The Network organizes speaking tours of Nicaraguans in the US and study tours and volunteer brigades to Nicaragua. Some important current campaigns are: confronting water privatization, debt cancellation for Nicaragua and other poor countries, and radical change of IMF/World Bank measures. We also have campaigns in support of unemployed coffee workers, banana workers, labor organizing in the Free Trade Zones, indigenous rights, and the efforts of Nicaraguan environmental organizations.

(Also listed under "Alternative Travel and Study Overseas")

Los Niños

287 G Street, Chula Vista, CA 91910
Tel: (619) 426-9110
Fax: (619) 426-6664
E-mail: info@losninosintl.org
Website: www.losninosinternational.org

Los Niños supports long-term community development projects along the US–Mexico border, and works with high schools and universities in Canada and the US. Program areas include nutrition, ecology, microcredit, cross-cultural issues, and education, and are designed to promote self-reliance and social awareness. Los Niños offers long-term volunteer opportunities to assist in these programs. Volunteers are expected to make a minimum commitment of one year. Interested candidates should send a resume to the above e-mail address. Los Niños has no religious or political affiliations.

(Also listed under "Alternative Travel and Study Overseas")

Nuestros Pequeños Hermanos International $ ⊗ ⊞

Mailing address: Apdo. Postal 333, 62000 Cuernavaca, Morelos, Mexico
Tel: + (52) 777-311-4600
Fax: + (52) 777-311-5152
E-mail: info@nph.org
Website: www.nph.org
To apply to volunteer at NPH:
Friends of the Orphans
1800 112th Avenue NE, Suite 308-E, Bellevue, WA 98004
E-mail: volunteers@friendsus.org
Website: www.friendsoftheorphans.org

Nuestros Pequeños Hermanos is a charitable organization serving orphaned and abandoned children in Latin America and the Caribbean. Its mission is to provide shelter, food, clothing, healthcare, and education in a Christian family environment based on unconditional acceptance and love, sharing, working, and responsibility.

NPH has homes in the Dominican Republic, El Salvador, Mexico, Honduras, Guatemala, Haiti, Nicaragua, Bolivia, and Peru.

Volunteers are asked to give a minimum of one year and may serve in a variety of positions, including as house parents, nurses, physicians, therapists, teachers, secretaries, gardeners, kitchen help, librarians, or assistants in the clinics.

Because of the difficulties that surround training, language, and accommodations for short-term volunteers, most positions require a strict commitment to one year of service. There are short-term (two to three months) volunteer opportunities in Haiti (July–August) and the Dominican Republic (June–August). Summer projects may involve volunteers in teaching English, music, dance, athletics, and arts and crafts. Volunteers must be at least 21 years old and in good health. Job placement in the Latin American homes will depend a great deal on degree of fluency in Spanish.

The children and staff at the orphanage in Haiti speak

Creole, while French is taught in the schools. At the hospital, a minimal knowledge of French is needed to communicate with the doctors and staff upon arrival. Creole is not a difficult language and each volunteer is expected to study it during the first weeks in Haiti. Most volunteers can learn enough Creole in their first two months to communicate with the children and staff.

Room and board is provided for all volunteers. Volunteers are expected to pay travel expenses to and from the country assignment. A small monthly stipend is given to full-time volunteers in Mexico, Honduras, Haiti, Nicaragua, Guatemala, and the Dominican Republic.

Operation Crossroads Africa

34 Mount Morris Park West, New York, NY 10027
Tel: (212) 289-1949
Fax: (212) 289-2526
E-mail: oca@igc.org
Website: www.operationcrossroadsafrica.org

Established in 1957, Operation Crossroads Africa oversees two volunteer programs: the Africa program, which annually supports 15 to 20 work projects in Africa, and the Diaspora program, which focuses on Brazil because of its large Afro-Brazilian population. Crossroads programs run in the following African countries: Benin, Botswana, Burkina Faso, Ethiopia, The Gambia, Ghana, Kenya, Lesotho, Malawi, Mali, Namibia, Senegal, South Africa, Tanzania, and Uganda. The Crossroads summer program consists of three orientation days in New York City, six weeks of service on a rural project, and one week of travel in the host country. All Crossroads ventures are community initiated, and volunteers live and work with hosts who have designed the project. Among the possible assignments are construction of community facilities, public health drives, reforestation, and teaching. Specialized skills in medicine, construction, or local languages are welcome but not necessary.

The fee to participate is $3,500, exclusive of transportation to and from New York. Successful participation requires an interest in Africa and the Diaspora, strong communication skills, a desire to establish meaningful contact with people of other cultures, and a willingness to respect different beliefs and values. Many volunteers have been able to arrange academic credit for their service with Crossroads.

Peace Brigades International (PBI)

1326 9th Street NW, Washington, DC 20001
Tel: (202) 232-0142
Fax: (202) 232-0143
E-mail: info@pbiusa.org
Website: www.peacebrigades.org

PBI practices an effective approach to human rights protection known as protective accompaniment. PBI fields teams of international volunteers trained in nonviolence to accompany individuals and organizations facing death threats as a result of their work on behalf of human rights and social justice. PBI's work, based on the principles of nonviolence, nonpartisanship, and noninterference in the affairs of the groups they accompany, also includes intensive networking with local, national, and international officials; distribution of human rights information to the international community; and public education in the US and other countries.

PBI currently has projects in Colombia, Guatemala, Indonesia, Mexico, and Nepal.

Prospective volunteers attend a seven to ten day training before final selections are made. Participants must be willing to commit one year to 18 months of field service. Candidates for Latin America projects must be fluent in Spanish, and candidates for Indonesia and Nepal must be fluent in English and conversant in or willing to learn Bahasa Indonesian (for the Indonesia Project) or Nepali (for the Nepal Project). Upon acceptance, PBI covers travel, housing, food, health insurance, and other work-related expenses, in addition to a modest monthly stipend.

Peacework

209 Otey Street, Blacksburg, VA 24060-7426
Tel: (800) 272-5519 *or* (540) 953-1376
Fax: (540) 953-0300
E-mail: mail@peacework.org
Website: www.peacework.org

Peacework manages two kinds of international volunteer service programs:

1. Peacework short-term volunteer service projects around the world, in cooperation with indigenous relief and development organizations. Projects are normally organized for groups, which can include people from colleges, universities, civic, medical, or professional organizations. Orientation and interaction with the host community is a vital part of the program. Volunteers may provide hands-on assistance building houses, repairing orphanages, schools, and health facilities. Volunteers may also provide direct medical services, or be involved in health education, school tutoring, environmental efforts, wildlife conservation, and other projects with a local community. International experience, building skills, volunteer service, and foreign language proficiency are helpful but not required.

2. The Peacework Village Network is a partnership of universities and colleges with villages in countries of the global south, in which all of the departments and programs of one university are simultaneously engaged with their counterparts in one host community. Business students and faculty work with local enterprises and business education, while students and faculty in education work with schools and teachers and literacy. At the same time, those in engineering, social work, health care, political science, law, and other

fields become engaged with their counterparts in a collaborative, multidisciplinary development initiative. Building on this, the partnership quickly fosters similar initiatives and benefits throughout the region or even within an entire country. Peacework guides the process through planning, implementation, and evaluation, and provides all of the staffing and logistics.

Peacework services include local programming and planning with the host partner, international travel, visas and other documents, comprehensive liability and medical insurance, staffing as needed, all local support services, and 24/7 programmatic and emergency assistance. Project locations include Belize, Costa Rica, Honduras, the Dominican Republic, Ghana, Cameroon, Kenya, Malawi, South Africa, the Czech Republic, Slovakia, Ukraine, India, Nepal, and other countries.

Plenty International

PO Box 394, Summertown, TN 38483
Tel/Fax: (931) 964-4323
E-mail: plenty@plenty.org
Website: www.plenty.org

Founded in 1974, Plenty promotes the cooperative exchange of appropriate village-scale technologies, skills, and resources between people worldwide. Special focus is on projects to assist indigenous peoples. Volunteer placements are limited and are based primarily in Belize. Volunteers must pay all travel and living expenses. Long-term volunteers (three months or more) skilled in organic agriculture, midwifery, nutrition, or sustainable energy are most needed. Plenty also runs a summer program in Tennessee for disadvantaged inner city kids called "Kids to the Country" that uses volunteers as counselors.

Quest: Volunteers for Haiti $ 🎱

4602 Clemson Road, College Park, MD 20704
Tel: (301) 927-7118
E-mail: collegeparkrjm@aol.com *or* volunteer@rjm-us.org
Website: www.rjm-us.org

Quest: Volunteers for Haiti, a volunteer program sponsored by the Religious of Jesus and Mary, offers yearlong and summer opportunities in Gros Morne and Jean Rabel, Haiti. Volunteers share simple living with two or three members of Religious of Jesus and Mary while serving the poor in a variety of agricultural, medical, and educational ministries. Orientation, room and board, (medical insurance and a monthly stipend, for yearlong volunteers), and daily transportation are provided. Volunteers must pay their own transportation at the beginning and end of term to and from the Haiti site.

Service Civil International–International Voluntary Service (SCI-IVS) $ 🔲

US Branch of Service Civil International
5505 Walnut Level Road, Crozet, VA 22932
Tel/Fax: (206) 350-6585
E-mail: info@sci-ivs.org *or* sciinfo@sci-ivs.org
Website: www.sci-ivs.org

SCI is a voluntary service organization and peace movement with 37 branches and 45 partners worldwide. Founded in 1920, SCI organizes international volunteer projects all over the world in the belief that if people with different backgrounds and cultures learn to cooperate and work together, peace can be the result. SCI organizes short-term projects called "workcamps" and long-term (one to twelve months) projects in Africa, Asia, Europe, Latin America, and the US. Volunteers work on environmental, social, solidarity, and construction/maintenance projects and must be at least 16 years old for the US, 18 years old for Europe, and 21 years old for all others. Volunteers pay travel expenses and receive the benefit of room and board and accident insurance while on the project. The application fee for US camps is $80 and $195 for most overseas projects. Most camps take place from July to September and last two to four weeks.

Servicio Internacional para la Paz (SIPAZ)

PO Box 3584, Chico, CA 95927
Tel/Fax: (530) 892-0662
E-mail: info@sipaz.org
Mexico: Ave. Chilon No 8 San Cristobal de las Casas 29220 Chiapas, Mexico
E-mail: chiapas@sipaz.org

Organized at the invitation of Mexican church and human rights groups, SIPAZ is a coalition of North American, Latin American, and European organizations dedicated to supporting the peace process in Chiapas, and increasingly in Oaxaca and Guerrero. SIPAZ seeks long-term volunteers to help carry out its work. Tasks include developing and maintaining relationships with groups and individuals concerned in the conflict, monitoring both formal talks and independent initiatives, preparing updates and analysis on the ongoing peace process, designing workshops on nonviolence, and assisting with presence and accompaniment duties. Prospective volunteers must be fluent in Spanish, 23 years or older, and have prior international work experience. Candidates should be committed to nonviolence and must be comfortable working with faith-based groups. A commitment of at least one year is required.

VIA

(formerly Volunteers in Asia)
965 Mission Street, Suite 751, San Francisco, CA 94103
Tel: (415) 904-8033
E-mail: info@viaprograms.org
Website: www.viaprograms.org

Since 1963, VIA has served impoverished communities throughout Asia. Each year, VIA places approximately 40 volunteers in

China, Indonesia, Vietnam, Laos, Myanmar, and Thailand. Volunteer placements are one to twenty-four months long. While most VIA volunteers work as English teachers, some also work closely with a local nonprofit group as an English resource. Our programs are open to native English speakers who are either US citizens or residents.

Jessy Needham, Volunteer, VIA, 2003–2005

My two years as a VIA volunteer gave me a one-of-a-kind opportunity to develop an in-depth understanding of Vietnamese society and culture, start learning the language, and explore the country, all of which provided a strong foundation for my current work as a scholarship administrator for Vietnamese students who want to study in the US.

Visions in Action

2710 Ontario Road NW, Washington, DC 20009
Tel: (202) 625-7402
Fax: (202) 588-9344
E-mail: visions@visionsinaction.org
Website: www.visionsinaction.org

Visions in Action is a nonprofit organization that offers six-month and one-year volunteer positions in Mexico, South Africa, Tanzania, and Uganda. Positions are available with non-profit development organizations, research institutes, health clinics, community groups, and the media. The program features an orientation with language study followed by a home-stay in a local community. Volunteers for long-term programs must be at least 20 years old and have two years of college or equivalent work experience. A college degree is beneficial but not a requirement. The program is open to people of any nationality. Married couples are also encouraged to apply.

Program fees vary by country and cover housing, health insurance, medical evacuation insurance, orientation, local staff and in-country support, program administration, and a stipend. The average cost is $4,000. For those seeking short-term volunteer placement, Visions in Action also offers, in Mexico and Tanzania, a seven-week summer program and a three-week winter program for those at least 18 years old.

Voluntary Service Overseas (VSO) Canada

806–151 Slater Street, Ottawa, Ontario K1P 5H3, Canada
Tel: (888) VSO–2911 or (613) 234–1364
Fax: (613) 234–1444
E-mail: inquiry@vsocan.org
Website: www.vsocan.org

VSO Canada is an international development agency that works through professional volunteers who live and work at the heart of communities in 34 countries around the world. Working in partnership with local colleagues, they share their skills and expertise to help find long-term solutions to poverty.

VSO sees development as a process that empowers people and communities to fight disadvantage, take control of their future, and fulfill their potential. Human rights, including an education, a livelihood, health care, a safe environment, a say in the future, and equal access to opportunity, are all vital for development. VSO describes lack of access to these fundamental human rights as disadvantage. They work with many partners to fight disadvantage within the framework of their six development goals.

VSO recruits skilled and experienced professionals from a wide range of backgrounds including education, health, and business. VSO volunteers usually have a professional qualification in their field as well as a minimum of at least two years experience. Volunteers live and work at the heart of local communities, where they share their professional skills to help bring about lasting change. The nature of jobs varies greatly but almost all volunteers are involved in building the capacity of individuals and organizations.

Applicants should be over 19 years old and be citizens of Canada, the US, or Canadian permanent residents. Placements overseas are usually between one and two years, but shorter terms may be available depending on expertise and needs.

VSO welcomes applications from people with disabilities, and strives to enable them to fully participate. VSO provides financial support in many ways.

Volunteer Missionary Movement (VMM)

5980 West Loomis Road, Greendale, WI 53129-1824
Tel: (414) 423-8660
Fax: (414) 423-8964
E-mail: vmm@vmmusa.org
Website: www.vmmusa.org

VMM is a nonsectarian international community of Christians rooted in the Catholic tradition, which seeks—by sharing resources, skills, and lives—to challenge oppressive unjust structures and promote equality, respect, and dignity. VMM sponsors locally initiated programs in Africa (Ethiopia, Kenya, South Africa, Sudan, Tanzania, Uganda, and Zambia), Central America (El Salvador and Guatemala), and the US. The term of placement is a minimum of two years, and is open to anyone 23 years of age or older who can dedicate the time to serve. VMM asks potential volunteers to have at least one year's work experience, though some placements do require a technical or bachelor's degree. Where the project partner is amenable, VMM will work to place a volunteer with a disability.

VMM covers the cost of health insurance, training, travel to and from the mission site, language school, living stipend, and resettlement allowance. The project partner typically takes care of room and board. Out of a total placement cost of $17,000, the volunteer is expected to raise $6,000. VMM helps the volunteer develop a fund-raising plan to make it simple.

Volunteers For Peace, Inc. (VFP)

1034 Tiffany Road, Belmont, VT 05730
Tel: (802) 259-2759
Fax: (802) 259-2922
E-mail: vfp@vfp.org
Website: www.vfp.org

VFP recruits volunteers for over 3,400 international voluntary
service projects in 100 different countries (located in North,
Central, and South America; Asia, Africa, Europe, as well as
some Pacific Islands). At a project, also known as a workcamp,
10 to 20 people from five or more countries join together for
two to three weeks to support community projects in construction, restoration, environmental work, social services,
agriculture, and archaeology. In 2006 VFP exchanged over
1,000 volunteers. Volunteers arrange their own travel and pay a
registration fee of $250, which covers room and board for
the duration of most projects. Volunteers can participate in
multiple projects in the same or different countries. The VFP
International Workcamp directory, a listing of over 2,300
opportunities for travel, is available to download at the VFP
website. Call, write, or e-mail VFP for a free newsletter, which
includes many reports and photos from their projects.

Witness for Peace (WFP)

3628 12th Street, NE, 1st Floor, Washington, DC 20017
Tel: (202) 547-6112
Fax: (202) 536-4708
E-mail: witness@witnessforpeace.org
Website: www.witnessforpeace.org

Volunteers with WFP work with communities in Colombia,
Mexico, Nicaragua, and Venezuela, making a two-year commitment. Long-term volunteers document human rights abuses,
study the effects of North American foreign and economic policies on the region, provide sociopolitical analyses of domestic
affairs, facilitate short-term delegations of North Americans,

and stand with the people in the spirit of international awareness and the ethos of nonviolence as a means for positive social
change. Volunteers must be US citizens and fluent in Spanish.
Volunteers pay costs of roundtrip airfare and attempt to raise
$1,000 for WFP to help cover living expenses. WFP provides
training, room and board, medical, a monthly stipend, and a
roundtrip plane ticket to the US after the first year of service.

WorkingAbroad Projects

United Kingdom: PO Box 454, Flat 1, Brighton BN1 3ZS, East Sussex, UK
France: 7 rue d'Autan, 11290 Montreal d'Aude, France
Tel/Fax: + 0033 468 264179
E-mail: info@workingabroad.com
Website: www.workingabroad.com

WorkingAbroad Projects is a nonprofit that provides volunteer
assistance to small-scale organizations on request. The aim is to
create small, independent, and effective projects that directly
engage grassroots organizations in these focus areas: cultural
development, earth restoration, permaculture, indigenous
rights, and traditional arts and music. WorkingAbroad Projects
has programs in Costa Rica, the Netherlands Antilles, and
Iceland. Volunteers should be at least 18 years old and culturally aware. The costs for programs range from free room and
board to $1,480, which includes room and board, materials,
training, and local transportation.

(Also listed under "Resources")

World Bridges (WB)

1203 Preservation Park, Suite 301, Oakland, CA 94612
Tel: (510) 451-2995
Fax: (510) 451-2996
E-mail: info@world-bridges.org
Website: www.world-bridges.org

WB's mission is to promote peace and justice by creating
opportunities for diverse young people from low-income back-

grounds to collaborate, raise awareness, and take action both locally and globally. Through leadership development, participatory trainings, and international exchanges, WB provides a continuum of experiences that nurture personal growth and empower participants to build alliances across communities and cultures.

The Leadership Exchange Program supports diverse youth in the US—primarily from low-income backgrounds—in gaining the experience, knowledge, and skills required to be effective, globally minded leaders in multicultural and international environments. Through unique service-learning and alliance-building activities, participants gain understanding of the US role in global affairs and of their individual connections to the global community.

WorldTeach, Inc.

Center for International Development, Harvard University
79 John F. Kennedy Street, Cambridge, MA 02138
Tel: (800) 483-2240 *or* (617) 495-5527
Fax: (617) 495-1599
E-mail: info@worldteach.org
Website: www.worldteach.org

WorldTeach is a nonprofit, nongovernmental organization based at the Center for International Development at Harvard University. Founded in 1986, WorldTeach provides opportunities for individuals to make a meaningful contribution to international education by living and working as volunteer teachers in countries of the global south. Volunteers teach English and other subjects to students of a variety of ages. Currently, teachers are needed in: Chile, China, Costa Rica, Ecuador, Guyana, the Marshall Islands, Namibia, Pohnpei, Poland, and South Africa. A bachelors degree (or equivalent) is required for 10 to 12 month teaching assignments; volunteers must be 18 years or older for summer programs. No previous language or teaching experience is necessary. Room and board are provided during the period of service for all volunteers; volunteers in long-term programs also receive a small monthly living allowance. The program fee for WorldTeach varies by country, ranging from fully funded to $5,990. Some countries are able to cover most of the cost of recruiting, placing, training, and supporting volunteer teachers. Others must rely on volunteers to contribute or fundraise the cost of their placement and support. By requesting that volunteers help fund their service overseas, WorldTeach is able to provide volunteer educators to countries that would not otherwise be able to afford qualified teachers. Program fees cover predeparture preparation (including visa), international airfare, insurance, training and orientation, an in-country field director, and after-service support and networking. Student loans may be deferred during the term of service. Applications are accepted on a rolling admissions basis and may be printed from the WorldTeach website or requested by contacting the WorldTeach admissions office.

Molly Moran, Volunteer, WorldTeach

My experience in Namibia has been one that I will never forget. Nothing is ever routine. The only constant is that every day offers new surprises and challenges. I believe I have learned more about life from the children I teach than they have learned from me. Our cultures are so different, and yet the basics are the same. You smile when you are happy, cry when you are sad, and eat when you are hungry. The smiles that we exchange numerous times a day mean more to them than a brand new pair of Nikes! I have made wonderful friends here whom I will never forget, and hope to continue to learn from them and carry on our friendships wherever we may be. As long as you have an open mind and an open heart, everything else falls into place.

5

US Voluntary Service Organizations

Working overseas is not the only way to gain community development experience. In many areas of the US, people face conditions of poverty similar to those found in other countries. Voluntary service in the US can offer a low-cost opportunity for building solid credentials toward a career in community development.

One of the best resources for domestic volunteering may well be your local yellow pages, under Social Service Organizations. Here are some organizations that recruit nationally and perform admirable work.

Bikes Not Bombs (BNB)

284 Amory Street, Jamaica Plain, MA 02130
Tel: (617) 522-0222
Fax: (617) 522-0922
E-mail: mail@bikesnotbombs.org
Website: www.bikesnotbombs.org

BNB is a nonprofit grassroots development and solidarity organization that uses bicycles for development work overseas and also for youth programs and community environmental action in the Boston area. Since 1984 BNB has helped local groups form ecologically viable bicycle workshops and related projects in Central America, the Caribbean, and Africa. These projects have involved collecting and shipping over 26,000 donated bicycles and tons of parts. BNB is currently sending bikes and parts to the Maya Pedal organization (Guatemala), the Village Bicycle Project (Ghana), the El Salvadoran Center for Appropriate Technology, a new bike shop and youth program in Diepsloot, South Africa, and Nevis Island. Past shipments have also gone to Nicaragua, Haiti, the Dominican Republic, and the Plan-B bicycle program in New Orleans. BNB's local youth Earn-A-Bike program (where youth learn mechanics and riding skills while rebuilding a bicycle of their own) is now replicated in Ghana, South Africa, and Nevis Island. Besides bicycle shipments, BNB provides technical assistance, training, tools, and sometimes financing for these projects. In the Boston area, BNB runs many youth programs, including Earn-A-Bike. Interns can work in Boston with youth programs, event planning, transportation and environmental activism, bike mechanics, or on computer and web issues.

Experienced bilingual mechanics with business or alternative technology skills, or youth with mechanical skills, are occasionally placed overseas to assist projects, launch bike shops, or run Earn-A-Bike programs. Every February BNB conducts mechanics classes for adults who, after teaching youth in Boston, may qualify to work overseas. BNB also runs a retail bike shop which serves as a job-training center for teens.

Casa de Proyecto Libertad (PL)

113 North First Street, Harlingen, TX 78550
Tel: (956) 425-9552
Fax: (956) 425-8249

PL promotes and defends the human rights of the border communities in South Texas through immigration legal services,

advocacy, and community organizing. PL's legal programs
include the NACARA Project, the Violence Against Women Act
(VAWA) Project, and representation in immigration court and
with the USCIS. PL works with political asylum, temporary
protected status, naturalization, and family visa applicants. PL
also facilitates the emergence of grassroots community organizations whose members are impacted by immigration laws and
enforcement policies. PL provides human rights trainings as
one step toward self-determination and social change. There
are volunteer opportunities in the legal and community organizing programs for those who speak Spanish and are sensitive
about cultural differences. Volunteers pay their own expenses,
but some assistance may be available.

Catholic Worker Movement (CW)

The Catholic Worker
36 East First Street, New York, NY 10003
Tel: (212) 777-9617
Website: www.catholicworker.org

The Catholic Worker Movement has 165 locations throughout
the US and Canada, as well as 16 international locations. There
is no national Catholic Worker headquarters. However, for a
copy of or subscription to *The Catholic Worker* newspaper, you
may contact the address above. Founded by Dorothy Day and
Peter Maurin in 1933, the Catholic Worker Movement is
grounded in the firm belief in the God-given dignity of every
person. CW communities are committed to nonviolence, voluntary poverty, and hospitality for the homeless, exiled, hungry, and forsaken. Houses are independent of one another and
vary in their activities and relationship to the Catholic Church,
and in how they incorporate Catholic Worker philosophy and
tradition. Most are based on the Gospel, prayer, and Catholic
beliefs, but some are interfaith. Catholic Workers live a simple
lifestyle in the community, serve the poor, and resist war and
social injustice. Most houses need volunteers; contact the house

you are interested in directly for further information. The national CW website maintains a complete list of community houses.

Center for Third World Organizing (CTWO)

1218 East 21st Street, Oakland, CA 94606
Tel: (510) 533-7583
Fax: (510) 533-0923
E-mail: ctwo@ctwo.org
Website: www.ctwo.org

CTWO is an organizing and training center that tackles issues affecting third-world communities throughout the United States. Community Action Training (CAT) is conducted in the spring, prior to the eight-week Minority Activists Apprenticeship Program (MAAP). MAAP provides training and field experience in techniques of community organizing for young people of color (primarily college students) who are working for social justice. Volunteers receive housing and a stipend. Other internships are sometimes available, including research and writing for partnership programs.

Citizen Action of New York

94 Central Avenue, Albany, NY 12206
Tel: (518) 465-4600, ext. 115
Fax: (518) 465-2890
E-mail: kcampbell@citizenactionny.org
Website: www.citizenactionny.org

Citizen Action of New York (a state affiliate of US Action) works at the grassroots level for racial, social, economic, and environmental justice across New York State. Volunteers work on one of the four current issue campaigns (Education, After-School, Health Care, or Clean Money/Clean Elections) in offices located in New York City, Buffalo, Binghamton, Long Island, Brooklyn, Syracuse, and Albany. Volunteers usually work with Citizen Action for a semester or a summer and are required to have some knowledge of American government. Interns and volunteers are expected to pay all living and transportation expenses. Paid internship opportunities occasionally arise based on foundation or grant support and are posted regularly on the website.

Council for Responsible Genetics (CRG)
5 Upland Road, Suite 3, Cambridge, MA 02140
Tel: (617) 868-0870
Fax: (617) 491-5344
E-mail: crg@gene-watch.org
Website: www.gene-watch.org

CRG is a nonprofit organization fostering public debate about the social, ethical, and environmental implications of genetic technologies. CRG works through the media and concerned citizens to distribute accurate information and represent the public interest on emerging issues in biotechnology. Primary program areas include genetic privacy and discrimination, biological warfare, genetically modified foods, human genetic modification, and reproductive technologies.

Four core principles drive the organization's work:

1. The public must have access to clear and understandable information on technological innovations.

2. The public must be able to participate in public and private decision making concerning technological developments and their implementation.

3. New technologies must meet social needs.

4. Problems rooted in poverty, racism, and other forms of inequality cannot be remedied by technology alone.

Unpaid internships are available during the summer and during the academic year. Interns should be qualified undergraduate and graduate students interested in bioethics and emerging biotechnologies. Opportunities include working with senior staff and board members on individual research, writing, or outreach projects in specific program areas.

Food First/Institute for Food and Development Policy
(See description of Food First at the back of this book)

The Food Project
PO Box 705, Lincoln, MA 01773
Tel: (781) 259-8621
Fax: (781) 259-9659
E-mail: participate@thefoodproject.org
Website: www.thefoodproject.org

The Food Project's mission is to create a thoughtful and productive community of youth and adults from diverse backgrounds working together to build a sustainable food system. The Food Project's farms in Boston and Lincoln produce healthy food for residents of the city and its suburbs, provide youth leadership opportunities, and inspire and support others to create change in their own communities. Volunteers help on both farms from April through June and from late August through mid-November. They learn about sustainable agricultural practices and food-systems, as well as food-security issues. Volunteers work from one to three days per week through the growing season. No previous farming experience is required. Volunteers must be at least 15 years old and those under 18 years old must have parental consent to work. Occasionally there are volunteer opportunities in other programs.

InterConnection
2222 North Pacific Street, Seattle, WA 98103
Tel: (206) 310-4547 *or* (866) 621-1068
Fax: (206) 633-1517
E-mail: info@interconnection.org
Website: www.interconnection.org

InterConnection provides nonprofits and NGOs in countries of the global south with websites, computer and Internet training, and refurbished computers. Though the work may take a volunteer virtually to a country in South and Central America or Africa, because volunteers don't leave home, there aren't any accessibility issues. The only requirement is that volunteers be computer skilled and web savvy. The average time commitment for a placement is one month. Volunteers will incur no costs.

Lutheran Volunteer Corps (LVC)

1226 Vermont Avenue NW, Washington, DC 20005
Tel: (202) 387–3222
Fax: (202) 667–0037
E-mail: recruitment@lutheranvolunteercorps.org
Website: www.lutheranvolunteercorps.org

LVC is a Reconciling in Christ Organization. LVC volunteers work in advocacy and public policy, AIDS/HIV, community development and organizing, education, the environment, food and hunger, health care, housing, immigration and refugee services, legal assistance, social and direct services, shelters, and programs for women and youth. Placements are in Baltimore, MD; Wilmington, DE; Washington, DC; Chicago, IL; Milwaukee, WI; Minneapolis/St. Paul, MN; Seattle and Tacoma, WA; and Oakland/Berkeley, CA. Volunteers live communally with three to six other volunteers, commit to a simplified lifestyle, and work for social justice. Travel, room and board, medical coverage, and daily work-related transportation expenses are covered. The program is open to people of all faiths and ages. Married couples and couples in committed partnerships are welcome to apply.

National Coalition for the Homeless (NCH)

2201 P Street NW, Washington, DC 20037-1033
Tel: (202) 462-4822, ext. 19
Fax: (202) 462-4823
E-mail: mstoops@nationalhomeless.org
Website: www.nationalhomeless.org

NCH works to create the systematic and attitudinal changes necessary to prevent and end homelessness through grassroots organizing, public education, policy advocacy, lobbying, litigation, and technical assistance. NCH also works to meet the immediate needs of those who are homeless or at risk of becoming homeless. Its first principle of practice is getting those who have experienced homelessness involved in all aspects of the organization's work.

Each year NCH offers a limited number of volunteer/internship opportunities. Generally interns are assigned to one of the issue areas of NCH's work: civil rights, health, affordable housing, income, media/publications, or community organizing. Internships last from three weeks to a year. Many of NCH's interns are currently undergraduate or graduate students, or have recently graduated. However, others are encouraged to apply. Though interns are expected to pay for their own expenses, students should check with their universities about the possibility of receiving school credit or a stipend.

Pesticide Action Network North America (PANNA)

49 Powell Street, Suite 500, San Francisco, CA 94102
Tel: (415) 981-1771
Fax: (415) 981-1991
E-mail: skegley@panna.org
Website: www.panna.org

PANNA works to replace pesticide use with ecologically sound and socially just alternatives. As one of five Pesticide Action Network regional centers worldwide, the San Francisco office links local and international consumer, labor, health, environment, and agriculture groups into an international citizens' action network. This network challenges the global proliferation of pesticides, defends basic rights to health and environmental quality, and works to ensure the transition to a just and viable society. PANNA accepts volunteers on a year-round basis. Projects and length of time vary depending on the program's needs.

Service Civil International
(See listing under "International Voluntary Service Organizations")

South Dakota General Convention of Sioux YMCAs   ⚇
PO Box 218, Dupree, SD 57623
Tel: (605) 365-5232
Fax: (605) 365-5230
E-mail: crandall@siouxymca.org
Website: www.siouxymca.org

The Sioux YMCAs are the only Ys in the US on Indian reservations. The location on the Cheyenne River Sioux Reservation mostly serves Lakota Sioux families. They offer two types of volunteer opportunities for college-aged or older participants. Volunteers may serve for two months during the summer as staff at YMCA Camp Leslie Marrowbone, working with children between the ages of 7 to 14 years. They also need community development volunteers to live in Dupree while supporting various youth and family programs. These placements last three months to one year. Volunteers must have camp or community work skills, and be flexible and open to a new culture. Both positions provide housing and a stipend.

United Farm Workers of America (UFW)

PO Box 62, Keene, CA 93531
Tel: (661) 823-6105
Fax: (661) 823-6174
E-mail: execoffice@ufw.org
Website: www.ufw.org

UFW works for justice for farm workers and safe food for consumers. They are now conducting the largest agricultural worker organizing campaign in over 20 years. UFW is seeking talented and motivated organizers to be part of this groundbreaking campaign in California. Prospective candidates must speak Spanish, and UFW prefers those who have bilingual writing abilities. UFW offers competitive salaries and benefits, depending on an applicant's prior experience.

Volunteer Missionary Movement (VMM)

(See listing under "International Voluntary Service Organizations")

6

ALTERNATIVE TRAVEL AND
STUDY OVERSEAS

IN THIS SECTION YOU WILL FIND SHORTER–TERM VOLUN-
teer opportunities, as well as options for travel to unusual destinations. A brief work stint with one of the organizations listed
here (such as a two-week excursion building a well in Nicaragua
with El Porvenir) can acquaint you with living in another country and help you decide if a long-term commitment makes
sense for you. A number of groups conduct "reality tours," study
tours, or delegations in countries of the global south and the
US. These are meant to be socially responsible educational
tours that provide participants with firsthand experience of the
political, economic, and social structures that create or sustain
hunger, poverty, and environmental degradation. Tour participants meet with people from diverse sectors with various perspectives on issues of agriculture, development, and the
environment. They often stay with local people, visit rural
areas, and meet with grassroots organizers. The experience and
insights gained on such a tour may influence participants'
future work for democratic social change. Many universities
offer study-abroad programs. This section mentions just a few
of them.

Amizade, Ltd.

(See listing under "International Voluntary Service Organizations")

Bike-Aid

Global Exchange
2017 Mission Street, Second Floor, San Francisco, CA 94110
Tel: (415) 255-7296 *or* (800) RIDE-808
E-mail: bikeaid@globalexchange.org
Website: www.globalexchange.org

Bike-Aid is a cross-country cycling trip sponsored by Global Exchange, a nonprofit human rights organization working for global political, economic, environmental, and social justice. Bike-Aid combines physical challenge, community interaction, global education, leadership, fundraising, and service learning. There are summer trips across the country, two-week trips down the California coast, and a December ride through the Hawaiian Islands. Along the routes, participants can exchange information and get a firsthand look into local community groups, the issues that are facing them, and the solutions that are taking place. Overnight lodging includes organic farms, Native American Indian reservations or indigenous communities, churches, and camping. People from all backgrounds, ages, and abilities are encouraged to participate.

Bridges to Community

95 Croton Avenue, Ossining, NY 10562
Tel: (914) 923-2200
Fax: (914) 923-8396
E-mail: info@bridgestocommunity.org
Website: www.bridgestocommunity.org/

Bridges to Community is a nonprofit cultural exchange organization that takes volunteers to countries in the global south to work, learn, and reflect. Through the process of living and working with local communities on construction, health, and environmental projects, they promote cross-cultural learning, a deepening awareness of our global interdependence and a commitment to the common good. Bridges to Community has brought more than 4,000 North American volunteers to Nicaragua since 1993. Most trips to Nicaragua are nine days in length, and include an orientation upon arriving in the host country, the experience of living in and working with a local community, and a little sightseeing. Volunteers find themselves sleeping on cots, eating staple foods, using outhouses, and most importantly, creating friendships that will lead to a greater sense of global community.

Center for Global Education, Augsburg College

2211 Riverside Avenue, Minneapolis, MN 55454
Tel: (800) 299-8889 *or* (612) 330-1159
Fax: (612) 330-1695
E-mail: globaled@augsburg.edu
Website: www.centerforglobaleducation.org

The Center for Global Education designs and coordinates travel seminars to Central America, Mexico, and Southern Africa. The goal is to foster critical analysis of local and global conditions so that personal and systemic change takes place. Participants meet with a wide range of representatives in government, business, church, and grassroots communities. Their focus is on sustainable development, human rights, women's roles, and the roles and responsibilities of people working for social change. They also arrange longer study programs for undergraduate students.

Center for Environmental Education and Ecological Action (CEDUAM)

(See listing under "International Voluntary Service Organizations")

Christian Peacemaker Teams (CPT)

(See listing under "International Voluntary Service Organizations")

Christians for Peace in El Salvador (CRISPAZ)

(See listing under "International Voluntary Organizations")

Co-op America Travel-Links

120 Beacon Street, Somerville, MA 02143-4370
Tel: (800) 648-2667
Fax: (617) 492-3720
E-mail: mj@tvlcoll.com

Travel-Links is a full-service travel agency that emphasizes responsible tourism and seeks to promote understanding and cooperation among people through nonexploitative travel.

Crooked Trails

PO Box 94034, Seattle, WA 98124
Tel: (206) 383-9828
Fax: (206) 320-0505
E-mail: info@crookedtrails.com
Website: www.crookedtrails.com

Crooked Trails is a nonprofit community-based travel organization helping people broaden their understanding of the planet and its diverse cultures through education, community development, and responsible travel. Crooked Trails works in conjunction with indigenous people around the world, facilitating cultural exchanges that allow visitors and hosts opportunities to share in each other's lives. Participants join in daily activities such as the design and construction of community centers and water and sewage systems, participating in Buddhist seminars, working in the fields during harvest or planting season, fishing, and teaching in village schools. Evenings are set aside for meetings with local elders, fireside chats, music, dance, crafts, and language lessons.

Cultural Restoration Tourism Project

700 Broderick Street, San Francisco, CA 94117
Tel: (415) 563-7221
E-mail: info@crtp.net
Website: www.crtp.net

The Cultural Restoration Tourism Project (CRTP) is a nonprofit organization established to provide communities around

Sue Kopman, Participant, Cultural Restoration Tourism Project

...The raw, majestic beauty of the place is indescribable; the mountains, rivers, and sky provide a setting that has to be one of the closest places to heaven on earth. The powerful, rugged nature of the land always bathed in a soft light inspired awe about the surroundings and a closeness to one another, the Nepali villagers/hosts ... Going to work each day was a marvel of discovery as we uncovered forgotten treasures and lost histories in the temple ... I felt I joined a sorority of like-minded souls who couldn't have been more generous and warm. Coming from all parts of the world, there was a great camaraderie and sharing. The leaders were attentive, warm, and open to ideas ... It couldn't be a more wonderful experience. I would recommend it to anyone. Being the oldest person on the trip was never an issue. There was always something to do for anyone's skill level. But the work was never busy work; it always served a purpose. The accommodations were very comfortable. The food was delicious and fresh. Cooking lunch with the Nepali women was a highlight —they can whip up some amazing meals over an open flame.

the world with a chance to restore cultural artifacts that are in danger of extinction. Programs hosted by CRTP are always community initiated. We help communities who want to help themselves, but do not have the resources to do it on their own. The restoration efforts aid communities in their sustainable development both environmentally and economically.

The Chairro Gompa Restoration Project is a volunteer vacation program in Nepal, working with an ancient Buddhist monastery. Participants socialize with the resident monk and learn about Nepali culture and rural life firsthand. They work for a portion of the day at the restoration site on projects like mud plastering, roofing, and wall-painting conservation, with daily opportunities to help local cooks prepare lunch. In the afternoons and days off, participants choose from activities such as community interaction (visiting a school and neighbors, helping a farmer), hikes, tours of sacred sites, relaxing, independent sightseeing, continuing work at the site, etc. The tour fee is $2495.00 for 12 days.

Earthwatch Institute

3 Clock Tower Place, Suite 100, Box 75, Maynard, MA 01754-0075
Tel: (800) 776-0188 *or* (978) 461-0081
Fax: (978) 461-2332
E-mail: info@earthwatch.org
Website: www.earthwatch.org

Earthwatch Institute is an international nonprofit organization that brings science to life for people concerned about the earth's future. Founded in 1971, Earthwatch supports scientific field research in more than 50 countries by offering volunteers the opportunity to join research teams. Today, Earthwatch recruits close to 4,000 volunteers every year to collect field data in the areas of climate change, ocean sustainability, rainforest ecology, wildlife conservation, archaeology, and more. Through this process, Earthwatch educates, inspires, and involves a diversity of people, who actively contribute to conserving our planet. Project teams last from one to two weeks and no special skills are required.

Explorations in Travel, Inc.

2458 River Road, Guilford, VT 05301
Tel: (802) 257-0152
Fax: (802) 257-2784
E-mail: explore@volunteertravel.com
Website: www.volunteertravel.com *or* www.exploretravel.com

Explorations in Travel provides individual volunteer work placements for students and adults from all over the world. Placements can be arranged in Belize, Costa Rica, Ecuador, Guatemala, and Puerto Rico. Work sites include schools, wildlife rehabilitation centers, animal shelters, and sustainable ecotourism projects. Language classes can be incorporated into a placement. Fees are from $700 to $975; there is a nonrefundable application fee of $35. Both individual and group programs are available. Explorations in Travel can also help with flight arrangements and fundraising ideas.

Fourth World Movement/USA
(See listing under "International Voluntary Service Organizations")

Global Citizens Network (GCN)
130 North Howell Street, St. Paul, MN 55104
Tel: (800) 644-9292 *or* (651) 644-0960
Fax: (651) 646-6176
E-mail: info@globalcitizens.org
Website: www.globalcitizens.org

GCN offers individuals the opportunity to interact with people of diverse cultures to develop creative and effective local solutions to global problems. GCN sends short-term teams of volunteers to communities in other countries, where they are partnered with a grassroots organization active in meeting community needs. Volunteers assist and work under the direction of local people on locally initiated projects, staying with host families or living as a group at a community center. Each team member receives training materials and participates in an orientation session. Groups are led by GCN team leaders.

Tours last one to three weeks, including travel time, and expenses run from $800 to $2200, excluding airfare. This covers most medical and evacuation insurance, training materials, a donation to the project, and a portion of program costs. Children ages 8 to 12 years old are half price, volunteers between the ages of 8 to 17 years must be accompanied by a parent or guardian. There is no upper age restriction. Returning former volunteers receive a discount as well. No specific skills are required. Project work ranges from school or road repair to water and sanitation projects to trail renovation. Current sites include Guatemala, Kenya, Mexico, Nepal, Tanzania, Thailand,

Brazil, Ecuador, Canada, and Native American reservations in Arizona, New Mexico, and Washington.

Global Exchange Reality Tours (GX)

2017 Mission Street, Suite 303, San Francisco, CA 94110
Tel: (415) 255-7296
Fax: (415) 255-7498
E-mail: realitytours@globalexchange.org
Website: www.globalexchange.org

GX organizes reality tours, study seminars, and human rights delegations to more than 25 countries. These study tours offer a unique opportunity to learn firsthand about pressing issues confronting the global south. Tour participants meet with peasant and labor organizers, community and religious leaders, peace activists, environmentalists, scholars, students, indigenous leaders, and government officials. Countries visited include Venezuela, Ecuador, Bolivia, Mexico, Cuba, Israel/Palestine, Iran, Vietnam, India, and Afghanistan. Costs range from $850 to $3,200. Their delegations provide an educational introduction to a country that often leads participants to develop connections with organizations where they can volunteer.

Heifer International, Study Tours

1 World Avenue, Little Rock, AR 72202
Tel: (800) 422-0474
E-mail: studytours@heifer.org
Website: www.heifer.org/studytours

Heifer International is a worldwide community development organization that provides farm animals, as well as training and related agricultural, environmental, and community-building services, to farmers in developing areas in 49 countries, including 23 states in the US. Heifer conducts 8- to 20-day study tours to its program areas. Groups meet Heifer in-country staff and learn about sustainable development and practical methods for caring for the earth. Heifer study tours, rather than being work trips, foster information gathering and critical thinking, so that participants return motivated to take action toward the Heifer vision: "A world of communities living together in peace and equitably sharing the resources of a healthy planet." Heifer trips range in cost from $2,000 to $6,000, and usually include international airfare (where applicable).

Ibike/Bicycle Africa

International Bicycle Fund (IBF)
4887 Columbia Drive South, Suite Q, Seattle, WA 98108-1919
Tel/Fax: (206) 767-0848
E-mail: ibike@ibike.org
Website: www.ibike.org/ibike

IBF promotes bicycle transportation, economic development, international understanding, and safety education. IBF arranges two- to four-week cultural immersion–educational bicycle tours in Benin, Cameroon, Eritrea, Ethiopia, The Gambia, Ghana, Kenya, Malawi, Mali, Senegal, South Africa, Tanzania, Togo, Tunisia, Uganda, Zimbabwe, Cuba, Ecuador, Guyana, Korea, Nepal, the US, and Vietnam. Area specialists accompany each program. Cycling is moderate and participants do not need to have extensive touring experience. Costs range from $900 to $2,500, not including airfare.

Institute for Central American Development Studies (ICADS)

United States: Dept. 826, PO Box 025216, Miami, FL 33102-5216 USA
Costa Rica: Apdo. 300-2050, San Pedro Montes de Oca, San Jose, Costa
   Rica, Centro America
Tel: + (506) 225-0508
Fax: + (506) 234-1337
E-mail: info@icads.org or info@icadscr.com
Website: www.icads.org or www.icadscr.com

ICADS is a center for study, research, and analysis of Central American social and environmental issues that offers four separate and unique study programs in Costa Rica and Nicaragua:

1. ICADS INTENSIVE SPANISH IMMERSION PROGRAM:
   This program offers 30 days of intensive Spanish language
   for 4 1/2 hours daily, five days a week in Costa Rica. Small
   classes (four students or less) are geared to individual
   needs. Extra lectures and activities emphasize environmental issues, economic development, education, and health
   care. ICADS offers optional afternoon internship placements in grassroots organizations, and group community
   service activities.

2. ICADS SEMESTER INTERNSHIP PROGRAM:
   This program offers three award-winning programs, fall
   and spring semesters, in Costa Rica and Nicaragua. The
   program is progressive and aimed at students who wish
   to work on social justice issues and on behalf of the poor,
   women, and the oppressed. Students receive full semester
   credit and participants gain experience and fluency while
   working in health clinics, schools, feeding centers, sustainable development organizations, fair trade and women's
   and agricultural cooperatives.

3. ICADS FIELD COURSE IN RESOURCE MANAGEMENT AND
   SUSTAINABLE DEVELOPMENT:
   This program offers an interdisciplinary semester program
   in Costa Rica focusing on development from ecological,
   socioeconomic perspectives. Semester includes: four weeks
   of intensive Spanish and urban issues; five weeks in the field
   in managed and natural ecosystems, learning methodolo-
   gies of field research in social and natural sciences (banana
   transnationals, traditional agriculture, community cooperatives, cloud forest and watershed management); and five
   weeks of independent research working in rural communities. Students can participate in fall and spring terms for
   academic credit.

4. ICADS SUMMER INTERNSHIP PROGRAM:
   This ten-week noncredit summer study program includes
   three weeks of Spanish language training, as well as aca-

demic lectures and field visits highlighting sociopolitical, cultural, and environmental issues. The language training and coursework are interactive, reality based, and include field trips to many sites within Costa Rica. During phase two of the program, students have the opportunity to choose among 50 different individual internship sites in Costa Rica. The aim of the ICADS summer internship program is to make learning an exciting and dynamic experience, while allowing the student to integrate as fully as possible into a Costa Rican community, to become as fluent in Spanish as possible, and to make a lasting contribution to an organization and/or community where she/he works and learns. Some Spanish is required.

Susan Smith, Participant, Spanish Program, Institute for Central American Development Studies

Across the street from the US Embassy is the neighborhood of Pavas, a slum of tin houses built on a mountain of trash. We crossed the creek on rotten planks and stared at the disgusting water. The smell was wretched and the sights saddening. Trash was organized and packed down to make stairs. We carried pieces of wood through the maze of broken homes and human filth. We are helping an organization whose objective is to give every child a bed.

We entered the people's houses and our mouths dropped at the lumpy dirt floors, the tin roofs with holes, and the "toilets" (only pots) in corners. People made big barrels into ovens. Naked children stared at us. Old people hid behind "windows" (cracks in walls). We built five beds in two hours in the oven-baking houses. Our feet fell through huge holes in "floors" (boards crossed together like puzzles). The hair in our noses curled from the stench. Now ten children can sleep off the floor.

International Partnership for Service-Learning and Leadership (IPSL)

815 2nd Avenue, Suite 315, New York, NY 10017
Tel: (212) 986-0989
Fax: (212) 986-5039
E-mail: info@ipsl.org
Website: www.ipsl.org

IPSL offers programs that integrate volunteer community service and formal academic study abroad for credit. Programs are available in the Czech Republic, Ecuador (Galapagos, Guayaquil, and Quito), the UK, France, India, Israel, Italy, Jamaica, Mexico, the Philippines, Russia, Scotland, Thailand, and the US (with Native Americans in South Dakota). Each location offers a variety of community service projects such as basic education, aid to the handicapped, women's issues, recreation, social welfare, and health. Costs range from $4,200 to $14,000 per term. Participants are primarily undergraduate students for summer, fall/spring, full-year, or January and August intersessions. IPSL also offers a one-year master's degree in international service in Jamaica or Mexico (first semester) and the UK (second semester and thesis).

Interreligious Foundation for Community Organization (IFCO)

Pastors for Peace
418 West 145th Street, 3rd Floor, New York, NY 10031
Tel: (212) 926-5757
Fax: (212) 926-5842
E-mail: ifco@igc.org
Website: www.ifconews.org *or* www.pastorsforpeace.org

Pastors for Peace is an action/education project of IFCO and includes activists from all sectors of society. Pastors for Peace organizes humanitarian aid caravans, work brigades, delegations, and study tours to Cuba, Central America, and Mexico. Churches, schools, and other organizations can name the dates and help define the itinerary of customized study tours and construction brigades for their members.

Marazul Charters, Inc.

8328 SW 40th Street, Miami, FL 33155
Phone: (305) 485-1203
Fax: (305) 559-8258
E-mail: miamicentral@marazulcharters.com
Website: www.marazul.com

Since 1979 Marazul has sent more than 300,000 people to Cuba. As a fully licensed travel service provider, Marazul assists licensed individuals and educational, religious, and humanitarian groups with all aspects of travel including air arrangements to Cuba on direct flights from Miami, as well as flights through third countries such as Canada, Mexico, the Bahamas, and Jamaica; Cuban visas; and land arrangements from accommodations and transportation to meetings, visits, and exchanges. Staff are bilingual in Spanish and English. A member of the American Society of Travel Agents, Marazul is a fully computerized, full-service travel agency.

Mexico Solidarity Network (MSN)

3460 W Lawrence Avenue, Chicago, IL 60625
Tel: (773) 583-7728
Fax: (773) 583-7738
E-mail: msn@mexicosolidarity.org
Website: www.mexicosolidarity.org

MSN is a network of US grassroots organizations supporting economic and social justice and democracy on both sides of the US-Mexico border. Their focus is on globalization and neoliberal economic policies that affect border communities as well as the indigenous population of Chiapas. MSN sponsors US speaking tours for Mexican activists, as well as university-accredited semester and summer study-abroad programs for US undergraduate and graduate students on Mexican social movements. In addition, MSN offers an alternative economy internship to support women's cooperatives in Chiapas.

Middle East Children's Alliance (MECA)

901 Parker Street, Berkeley, CA 94710
Tel: (510) 548-0542
Fax: (510) 548-0543
E-mail: meca@mecaforpeace.org
Website: www.mecaforpeace.org

MECA raises funds for humanitarian aid (medical supplies, school books, food, and clothing) for children in Iraq, the West Bank, and Gaza. For 16 years MECA has taken North Americans on 12- to 14-day trips into Israel and the Occupied Palestinian Territories (OPT) to see for themselves the effects of over 50 years of apartheid and occupation.

MECA's aim is to provide delegates with information about the current political situation as well as insights into the daily lives of people living under occupation and within the specter of Israeli apartheid. Their hosts are activists, academics, health-care workers, refugees, and international aid workers. By bearing witness, participants come away with a stronger understanding of the issues facing Palestinians in the OPT and Israel and are prepared to help others understand these issues.

(Also listed under "International Voluntary Service Organizations")

Minnesota Studies in International Development (MSID)

University of Minnesota, Learning Abroad Center
230 Heller Hall, 271 19th Avenue South, Minneapolis, MN 55455-0340
Tel: (612) 626-9000 *or* (888) 700-UOFM
Fax: (612) 626-8009
E-mail: UMabroad@umn.edu
Website: www.UMabroad.umn.edu

MSID is a credit-bearing study-abroad program that combines intensive classroom work with individualized internships and research opportunities in grassroots development and social change projects in rural and urban settings alike. MSID offers programs in Ecuador, India, Kenya, and Senegal, with three enrollment options at each site: academic year, fall semester, and spring semester. Juniors, seniors, college graduates, and graduate students are eligible to apply. Tuition and fees vary from site to site. Students with disabilities can often be accommodated.

Mobility International USA (MIUSA)
132 East Broadway, Suite 343, Eugene, OR 97401
Tel: (541) 343-1284 (voice/TTY)
Fax: (541) 343-6812
E-mail: info@miusa.org
Website: www.miusa.org

MIUSA's international exchanges specialize in leadership training, community service, cross-cultural experiential learning, and advocacy for the rights and inclusion of people with disabilities. These short-term group exchanges for youth, adults, and professionals with and without disabilities take place in the US and abroad. MIUSA has coordinated exchanges with Azerbaijan, Bulgaria, China, Costa Rica, East Asia, Germany, Italy, Japan, Mexico, Russia, the UK, and other countries. Activities include training seminars and workshops, adaptive recreational activities, cross-cultural communication, language classes, and volunteer service projects. Exchanges vary from ten days to three weeks in length. MIUSA's National Clearinghouse on Disability and Exchange (NCDE) provides additional information on international exchange, volunteer, and community service opportunities. NCDE staff can respond to inquiries on the range of opportunities available and on how people with disabilities can make these possibilities a reality.

Nicaragua Network
(See listing under "International Voluntary Service Organizations")

Los Niños
(See Listing under "International Voluntary Service Organizations")

our developing world (odw)

13004 Paseo Presada, Saratoga, CA 95070-4125
Tel: (408) 379-4431
Fax: (408) 376-0755
E-mail: odw@magiclink.net
Website: www.magiclink.net/~odw

The main focus of odw is to bring the realities of the global south and the richness of diverse cultures to North Americans through programs in schools, churches, and community groups. Once or twice a year odw takes a small group of travelers who want firsthand experience on a reality tour. Past destinations have included Cambodia, Cuba, Guatemala, Honduras, Laos, Mozambique, Nicaragua, the Philippines, South Africa, Vietnam, Zimbabwe, and indigenous Hawaii. odw has tours to Venezuela, Cambodia and Laos with a five day extra option to Vietnam. By providing opportunities to talk with peasants, workers, women's associations, health workers, co-op members, and youth, odw tours give participants a chance to learn about health, agrarian reform, human rights and educational campaigns, and economic and social planning. Tours are tailored to the interests of the participants. They also organize tours for students, teachers, and other groups when invited.

Plowshares Institute

PO Box 243, 809 Hopmeadow Street, Simsbury, CT 06070
Tel: (860) 651-4304
Fax: (860) 651-4305
E-mail: plowshares@plowsharesinstitute.org
Website: www.plowsharesinstitute.org

Plowshares traveling seminars initiate cross-cultural dialogue between people of the global north and global south. Participants commit to intensive preparation before departure and community education upon return. Trip itineraries include meetings with religious and civic leaders, homestay experiences, and visits to development projects. The institute plans two-week programs to several countries including Brazil, China, Cuba, Indonesia, Uganda, and South Africa.

El Porvenir

E 7294 Hemlock Road, North Freedom, Wisconsin 53951
Tel: (608) 544-2086
Fax: (916) 227-5068
E-mail: tom@elporvenir.org
Website: www.elporvenir.org

El Porvenir supports self-help sustainable development in poor rural communities in Nicaragua through funding and technical aid to community-requested water, sanitation, and reforestation projects. El Porvenir sponsors one- to two-week work trips and one-week educational tours to Nicaragua eight times per year. The cost of the educational tour is $1,200 per person, plus airfare to Nicaragua; the cost of the work trip is $950 for two weeks or $800 for one week, plus airfare. Work trip participants stay in modest hostels and work alongside community members to construct a project. Educational tours visit various El Porvenir project villages and engage in cultural and recreational activities. No Spanish or construction experience is required. Work groups are limited to ten people. All groups are accompanied at all times by bilingual El Porvenir staff.

School for International Training (SIT)

SIT TESOL Certificate Program
Kipling Road, PO Box 676, Brattleboro, VT 05302-0676
Tel: (802) 258-3510 or (800) 336-1616
Fax: (802) 258-3316
E-mail: tesolcert@sit.edu or admssions@sit.edu
Website: www.sit.edu

SIT prepares interculturally effective leaders, professionals, and citizens committed to responsible global citizenship. SIT offers masters programs in international education, language and culture, NGOs and civil society, peace and conflict transformation, social justice, socially responsible management, sustainable development, and teacher preparation.

The SIT TESOL certificate program is a 130-hour, intensive four-week course providing practical teacher training through demonstrations, lesson planning and analysis, practice teaching, and feedback. In some locations, practitioners may choose to study more extensively over a longer period. Certification sites include: Australia, Brazil, Costa Rica, Japan, Poland, Spain, Thailand, and the US. Visit the website for more information.

(Also listed under "Resources")

Ufufuo, Inc.

1225 Geranium Street NW, Washington, DC 20012
Tel: (202) 722-1461
Fax: (202) 723-5376
E-mail: hjconfer@worldnet.att.net
Website: http://ufufuo.home.att.net

Ufufuo, Inc. is a public charity that grew out of the church-rebuilding movement of the 1990s. Their interfaith and international volunteers rebuild damaged or destroyed churches, mosques, or synagogues in the US and overseas. They also recruit volunteers for disaster response and rebuilding in the US. In 2004 they rebuilt a damaged church in Kenya; in 2005 they worked on hurricane recovery in Wachula, Florida; in 2006 on Katrina recovery in Pass Christian, Mississippi; in 2005/6 they worked under the Mennonite Disaster Service (MDS); and in 2007 they worked with the Methodist Relief Center in Mt. Pleasant, South Carolina. International volunteers cover their own passport, visa, inoculation, and discretionary spending expenses, but scholarships cover on-site costs. All domestic volunteers are required to have health insurance and provide their own transportation to and from projects. International volunteers' health insurance is covered through Volunteers For Peace (VFP) international workcamps.

US Servas

1125 16th Street, Suite 201, Arcata, CA 95521-5585
Tel: (707) 825-1714
Fax: (707) 825-1762
E-mail: info@usservas.org
Website: www.usservas.org

US Servas fosters a more just and peaceful world by promoting appreciation of cultural differences through homestays and experiences in volunteered host communities. During short-term (two-night) stays, travelers share aspects of their home and community life while discussing concerns about social and international problems. Some hosts offer longer visits. The application consists of an interview, two character references, and an $85 membership fee.

Voices on the Border

Educational Delegations, Long-Term Field Volunteer Opportunities
3321 12th Street NE, Washington, DC 20017
Tel: (202) 529-2912
Fax: (202) 526-4611
E-mail: voices@votb.org
Website: www.votb.org

Voices on the Border brings together rural communities of former war refugees in El Salvador with concerned groups and individuals in the US. The relationships that form help sustain Salvadoran communities both spiritually and financially, and provide US participants with an essential perspective on a different world. Voices supports community organizing efforts that build grassroots power and development projects to help people meet their basic needs and create sustainable sources of income. Voices sponsors several delegations a year to El Salvador to meet these communities and Salvadoran social justice organizations. Voices on the Border has a long-term volunteer stationed in the rural Lower Lempa region of El Salvador, with a one- to two-year commitment. They also take interns in the Washington, DC, office.

World-Wide Opportunities on Organic Farms–USA (WWOOF–USA)

PO Box 432, Occidental, CA 95465
Tel: (831) 425-3276
E-mail: info@wwoofusa.org
Website: www.wwoofusa.org

WWOOF-USA's mission is to be a part of a worldwide effort to link volunteers with organic farmers, promote an educational exchange, and create a global community conscious of ecological farming practices. WWOOF is a purely voluntary program. Volunteers do not get paid; instead, they volunteer for half a day in exchange for room and board, provided by the farmer. Accommodations vary from farm to farm—anything from a tipi to a trailer, a room in a house, or tent space may be available. Duties will vary from farm to farm, and there are many different projects happening on various farms. To read the descriptions of the WWOOF host farms written by the farmers themselves, visit *www.wwoofusa.org* and click on "Preview WWOOF-USA Directory." There you can view the locations of all the host farms by city and state. There is no money exchanged, only knowledge, experience, and friendship. WWOOF-USA may also be contacted for information regarding volunteering with WWOOF internationally, or check *www.wwoof.org* for other countries with national programs and countries with independent WWOOF hosts.

7

Resources

OTHER ORGANIZATIONS

These groups do not generally sponsor internship or travel programs; they distribute information about volunteer or travel opportunities, foreign countries, underrepresented cultures, or aspects of development.

Bank Information Center (BIC)
1100 H Street NW, Suite 650, Washington, DC 20005
Tel: (202) 737-7752
Fax: (202) 737-1155
E-mail: info@bicusa.org
Website: www.bicusa.org

BIC provides hard-to-obtain information on the projects and policies of international funding institutions (like the World Bank) to environmental and social justice organizations in the global south. BIC offers numerous publications and reports and advocates for greater transparency in World Bank operations. There is much documentation here of the processes by which development is managed and mismanaged.

Center for Community Change (CCC)

1536 U Street NW, Washington, DC 20009
Tel: (202) 339-9300 *or* (877) 777-1536
E-mail: info@communitychange.org
Website: www.communitychange.org

For nearly four decades, the Center for Community Change has helped thousands of urban and rural communities nationwide organize for positive change by uniting low-income people across lines of race, ethnicity, geography, and gender to equip them with the tools to change public policies and demand public attention for issues of social and economic justice.

CIVICUS: World Alliance for Citizen Participation

24 Gwigwi Mrwebi Street (former Pim) corner Quinn Street, Newtown,
    2001 Johannesburg, South Africa
Tel: + (27) 11 833-5959
Fax: + (27) 11 833-7997
E-mail: info@civicus.org
Website: www.civicus.org

CIVICUS seeks to amplify the voices and opinions of ordinary people and it gives expression to the enormous creative energy of the burgeoning sector of civil society. CIVICUS: World Alliance for Citizen Participation is an international alliance of members and partners that constitutes an influential network of organizations at the local, national, regional, and international levels, and spans the spectrum of civil society, including trade unions and faith-based organizations, philanthropic foundations, businesses, and social responsibility programs. CIVICUS's membership currently includes members from almost 100 countries working to strengthen citizen action and civil society throughout the world, especially in areas where participatory democracy and citizens' freedom of association are threatened. CIVICUS has a vision of a global community of active, engaged citizens committed to the creation of a more just and equitable world. Its vision is premised on the belief that the health of societies exists in direct proportion to the degree of balance between the state, the private sector, and civil society. CIVICUS provides a focal point for knowledge-sharing, common-interest representation, global institution-building, and engagement among these disparate sectors. It acts as an advocate for citizen participation as an essential component of governance and democracy worldwide. CIVICUS produces a free weekly newsletter with invaluable information for civil society.

Cultural Survival, Inc.
215 Prospect Street, Cambridge, MA 02139
Tel: (617) 441-5400
Fax: (617) 441-5417
E-mail: culturalsurvival@cs.org
Website: www.cs.org

Cultural Survival, Inc., promotes the cause of self-determination for indigenous peoples worldwide, provides organizational support, and publishes reports on a host of topics relating to development.

Grassroots International
179 Boylston Street, 4th Floor, Boston, MA 02130
Tel: (617) 524-1400
Fax: (617) 524-5525
E-mail: info@grassrootsonline.org
Website: www.grassrootsonline.org

Grassroots International promotes global justice through partnerships with social change organizations. They work to advance political, economic, and social rights and support development alternatives through grant-making, education, and advocacy.

InterAction: American Council for Voluntary International Action

1400 16th Street, NW, Suite 210, Washington, DC 20036
Tel: (202) 667-8227
Fax: (202) 667-8236
E-mail: publications@interaction.org
Website: www.interaction.org

InterAction is the largest alliance of US-based international development and humanitarian nongovernmental organizations. With more than 160 members operating in every country in the global south, InterAction works to overcome poverty, exclusion, and suffering by advancing social justice and basic dignity for all. *Monday Developments*, a monthly newsletter, provides in-depth news and commentary on global trends that affect relief, refugee, and development work, and job opportunity listings throughout the world. InterAction also publishes *Member Profiles*, a biannual directory of its members; *Global Work*, a guide for volunteer, internship, and fellowship opportunities in international development abroad; and a weekly e-mail listing of extensive employment and internship opportunities in the international development and assistance field.

International Development Exchange (IDEX)

827 Valencia Street, Suite 101, San Francisco, CA 94110-1736
Tel: (415) 824-8384
Fax: (415) 824-8387
E-mail: info@idex.org
Website: www.idex.org

International Development Exchange (IDEX) is a nonprofit organization that promotes economic empowerment and social change in Africa, Asia, and Latin America. IDEX partners with community-based organizations to support their initiatives by providing grants, fostering regional and international alliances, and engaging US-based constituencies.

The International Ecotourism Society (TIES)
1333 H Street NW, Suite 300E, Washington, DC 20005
Tel: (202) 347-9203
Fax: (202) 789-7279
E-mail: info@ecotourism.org
Website: www.ecotourism.org

TIES is an international membership organization dedicated to disseminating information about ecologically sound and sustainable tourism. Individual memberships start at $35 per year and include subscription to the TIES newsletter, discounts on TIES publications, and access to lists of tour and lodge operators.

International Volunteer Programs Association (IVPA)
Foundation of Sustainable Development
31 73rd Street, Suite 2, North Bergen, NJ 07047
Tel: (201) 221-4105
E-mail: info@volunteerinternational.org
Website: www.volunteerinternational.org/ivpa

The International Volunteer Programs Association (IVPA) is a consortium of nongovernmental organizations that are involved in international volunteer and internship exchanges. In order to receive IVPA's distinguished seal of excellence, members are expected to uphold IVPA's principles and practices as guidelines for good programming as well as meet stringent membership criteria. IVPA stands for responsibility in the field of international volunteerism and promotes public awareness of and greater access to international volunteer programs. The IVPA website has a searchable database of volunteer opportunities as well as resources for prospective volunteers, student advisors, volunteer organizations, and corporations.

Panos Institute (PI)

Webster House, 1718 P Street, Suite T-6, Washington, DC 20036
Tel: (202) 429-0730 *or* (202) 429-0731
E-mail: panosinstitute@earthlink.net
Website: www.panosinst.org

PI specializes in news and research about development issues, and aims to stimulate public debate by providing accessible information on neglected or poorly understood topics as they affect the developing world, particularly in the fields of poverty, gender, environment, reproductive health, and population. PI publishes books, feature articles, briefings, and collected oral testimonies.

SANGONeT

PO Box 31392, Braamfontein, South Africa 2017
Tel: + (27 11) 403-4935
Fax: + (27 11) 403-0130
E-mail: info@sangonet.org.za
Website: www.sangonet.org.za

The Southern African NGO Network (SANGONeT) has been providing information communication technologies (ICT) services and solutions to the NGO sector in Southern Africa for the past 20 years. SANGONeT views ICTs as strategic tools that can build the capacity of organizations involved in development issues and the communities they serve. SANGONeT is the only Southern African NGO dedicated to providing an extensive range of ICT services to the local NGO sector, and is one of very few NGOs in Africa involved in ICT-related issues. Key SANGONeT activities include the SANGONeT NGO portal, annual ICT conference, Thetha ICT discussion forums, SANGOTeCH technology donation portal, and online PRODDER NGO directory.

School for International Training (SIT)

(See listing under "Alternative Travel and Study Overseas")

Transitions Abroad

18 Hulst Road, Amherst, MA 01002
Tel: (802) 442-4827
E-mail: info@transitionsabroad.com
Website: www.transitionsabroad.com

Transitions Abroad was founded in 1977 by Dr. Clay Hubbs to provide practical information on the alternatives to mass tourism: learning, living, working, volunteering, and vacationing with the people of the host country. The emphasis is on enriching, informed, affordable, and responsible travel. Transitions Abroad writers provide the details and "nuts and bolts" that their readers need to make their own plans. The magazine focuses on immediately usable practical information gained from firsthand experience, for readers who travel for something more than the sights.

Volunteers For Peace, Inc. (VFP)

(See listing under "International Voluntary Service Organizations")

WorkingAbroad Projects

(See listing under "International Voluntary Service Organizations")

GUIDES TO INTERNATIONAL VOLUNTARY SERVICE

How to Live Your Dream of Volunteering Overseas. Joseph Collins, Stefano DeZerega, and Zahara Heckscher (New York: Penguin Books, 2002). Penguin USA, 375 Hudson Street, New York, NY 10014-3657, Tel: (212) 366-2000, Fax: (212) 366-2666.

The International Directory of Voluntary Work, 10th edition. Victoria Pybus (Oxford: Vacation Work Publications, 2007). Distributed in the US by The Globe Pequot Press, 246 Goose Lane, PO Box 480, Guilford, CT 06437, Main Tel: (203) 458-4500, Customer Service Tel: (888) 249-7586, Fax: (800) 820-2329, Website: *www.globepequot.com.*

Social Change through Voluntary Action. M.L. Dantwala, Harsh
   Sethi, and Pravin Visaria (Thousand Oaks, CA: Sage
   Publications, Inc., 2000). Sage Publications, Inc., 2455 Teller
   Road, Thousand Oaks, CA 91320, Tel: (805) 499-0721,
   Website: *www.sagepub.com.*

GUIDES TO US VOLUNTARY SERVICE

Internships 2004 (Lawrenceville, NJ: Peterson's Guides, 2004).
   Peterson's Guides, PO Box 67005, Lawrenceville, NJ 08648,
   Tel: (800) 338-3282, Website: *www.petersons.com.*
*A World of Options: A Guide to International Educational
   Exchange and Travel for Persons with Disabilities.* Christa
   Bucks (Eugene, OR: Mobility International USA, 1997).
   Mobility International USA, 132 E Broadway, Suite 343,
   Eugene, OR 97440, Tel: (541) 343-1284.
The Global Activist's Manual: Local Ways to Change the World.
   Michael Prokosch, Laura Raymond, and Naomi Klein. (New
   York, NY, Nation Books 2002) Nation Books, 116 East 16th
   Street, 8th Floor, New York, NY 10003, Fax: 212-253-5356.

PUBLICATIONS ON TRAVEL AND TOURISM

Whether you intend to travel or volunteer abroad, the higher-
quality tourist guides can provide background on the history,
political situation, customs, and culture of countries or regions
that interest you. Check the travel section of your local book-
store or contact the publishers of the series below.

Travel Publishers

LONELY PLANET PUBLICATIONS, LONELY PLANET USA
   150 Linden Street, Oakland, CA 94607
   Tel: (510) 893-8555 Toll Free: 800 275 8555
   Fax: (510) 893-8572
   E-mail: info@lonelyplanet.com
   Website: www.lonelyplanet.com

Lonely Planet has an especially rich and detailed website, featuring bulletin boards, e-mail discussions, and up-to-the-minute information on numerous countries.

Moon Travel Handbooks (covering the Americas, Asia, and the Pacific)
Avalon Travel Publishing
1400 65th Street, Suite 250, Emeryville, CA 94608
Tel: (510) 595-3664 or (800) 285-4078
Fax: (510) 595-4228
Website: www.travelmatters.com or www.moon.com

Rough Guides USA
345 Hudson Street, 4th Floor, New York, NY 10014
Tel: (212) 414-3635
Website: www.roughguides.com

Travel Guides

Alternative Travel Directory: The Complete Guide to Work, Study and Travel Overseas, seventh edition. Clayton Hubbs and David Cline, ed. (Amherst, MA: Transitions Abroad Publishing, Inc., 2002). Transitions Abroad Publishing, 18 Hulst Road, PO Box 1300, Amherst, MA 01002, Tel: (413) 230-3597 and (413) 687-4273, Website: *www.transitionsabroad.com.*

Fodor's Great American Learning Vacations, 1997, second edition. (New York: Fodor's Travel Publications, 1997). Random House, 1745 Broadway, 3rd Floor, New York, NY 10019.

Free Vacations and Bargain Adventures in the USA. Evelyn Kaye (Boulder, CO: Blue Panda Publications, 1998). Blue Panda Publications, 3031 5th Street, Boulder, CO 80304.

Rethinking Tourism, second edition. Deborah McLaren (Bloomfield, CT: Kumarian Press, 2003). Kumarian Press, 1294 Blue Hills Avenue, Bloomfield, CT 06002, Tel: (800) 289-2664 or (860) 243-2098.

Transitions Abroad. Transitions Abroad Publishing, Inc., 18 Hulst Road, PO Box 1300, Amherst, MA 01002, Tel: (413) 256-3414, Website: *www.transitionsabroad.com.*

Volunteer Vacations: Short-Term Adventures That Will Benefit You and Others, 9th edition. Bill McMillon et al., eds. (Chicago, IL: Chicago Review Press, 2006). Chicago Review Press, 814 North Franklin, Chicago, IL 60610.

RESOURCES FOR FINDING JOBS IN DEVELOPMENT

Careers in International Affairs, 8th edition. School of Foreign Service (Washington, DC: Georgetown University Press, 2008). Georgetown University Press, 3240 Prospect Street, NW, Washington, DC 20007, Tel: (202) 687-5889, Website: *www.press.georgetown.edu.*

International Career Employment Weekly and *International Employment Hotline* (monthly). International Career Employment Center, Carlyle Corporation, PO Box 6729, Charlottesville, VA 22906-6729, Tel: (434) 985-6444, Fax: (434) 985-6828, E-mail: *Leo@mindspring.com,* Website: *www.internationaljobs.org.* Both publications contain extensive overseas job listings in the public and private sectors. Orientation is toward skilled professionals. The center also publishes an annual guide to overseas internships.

Work Abroad: The Complete Guide to Finding a Job Overseas 2002, fourth edition. (Amherst, MA: Transitions Abroad Publishing, Inc., 2002). Transitions Abroad Publishing, 18 Hulst Road, PO Box 1300, Amherst, MA 01002, Tel: (413) 256-3414, Website: *www.transitionsabroad.com.*

ONLINE RESOURCES

Association of Voluntary Service Organizations

Website: www.avso.org

Association of national and international nonprofits based in Europe. Site contains volunteer opportunities, links, and a bulletin board.

Grass-roots.org
Website: www.grass-roots.org
Lively descriptions of over 200 grassroots organizations in the US working in diverse and often innovative ways to eliminate poverty. Robin Garr, creator of the website, has also authored a book, *Reinvesting in America*, with many more program descriptions, along with a "Getting Involved" appendix list of groups that need volunteers.

Idealist (a project of Action without Borders)
Website: www.idealist.org
Lists thousands of volunteer opportunities and nonprofit jobs; offers publications and resources for nonprofits and consultants.

Project Cooperating for Cooperation
Website: www.coop4coop.org
Comprehensive directory of development organizations and volunteer programs.

FURTHER READING

Chasin, Barbara H. and Richard W. Franke. *Kerala: Radical Reform as Development in an Indian State.* Oakland, CA: Food First Books, 1994.

Chinn, Erica and Kristina Taylor, eds. *The Pros and Cons of the Peace Corps.* San Francisco, CA: Just Act.

CIVICUS. *Civil Society at the Millennium.* West Hartford, CT: Kumarian Press, 1999.

Collins, Joseph, Stefano DeZerega, and Zahara Heckscher. *How to Live Your Dream of Volunteering Overseas.* New York: Penguin Books, 2002.

Collins, Joseph, Frances Moore Lappé, and Peter Rosset, with Luis Esparza. *World Hunger: Twelve Myths.* New York: Grove Press, 1998.

Etzioni, Amitai. "How Not to Squander the Volunteer Spirit," *The Christian Science Monitor*, January 27, 2003, p. 11.

Fischer, Fritz. *Making Them Like Us: Peace Corps Volunteers in the 1960s*. Washington, DC: Smithsonian Institution Press, 1998.

Kutzner, Patricia L. and Nicola Lagoudakis, with Teresa Eyring. *Who's Involved with Hunger: An Organization Guide for Education and Advocacy*. Washington, DC: World Hunger Education Service, 1995.

Lappé, Frances Moore and Rachel Schurman. *Taking Population Seriously*. Oakland, CA: Food First Books, 1990.

MacMartin, Charley. "Peace Corps and Empire," *Covert Action Quarterly*, Winter 1991–1992, no. 39.

Razzi, Elizabeth. "One Pledge Fits All," the *San Francisco Chronicle*, November 29, 2002, p. A 28.

Reeves, T. Zane. *The Politics of the Peace Corps and VISTA*. Tuscaloosa, AL: University of Alabama Press, 2002.

"Russia, Citing Changing Needs, Ends Its Tie with Peace Corps," *The New York Times*, December 28, 2002, p. A4.

Shahinian, Mark. "Healing Africa: Peace Corps Plan Not Enough," *Milwaukee Journal Sentinel*, September 3, 2002, p. 13A.

Zimmerman, Jonathan. "Beyond Double Consciousness: Black Peace Corps Volunteers in Africa, 1961–1971," *Journal of American History*, December 1995, vol. 82, no. 3.

Alphabetical Index

Geographical Index

SOUTH AMERICA, CENTRAL AMERICA, CARIBBEAN

ABOUT FOOD FIRST

FOOD FIRST, also known as the Institute for Food and Development Policy, is a nonprofit research and education-for-action center dedicated to investigating and exposing the root causes of hunger in a world of plenty. It was founded in 1975 by Frances Moore Lappé, author of the bestseller *Diet for a Small Planet*, and food policy analyst, Dr. Joseph Collins. Food First research has revealed that hunger is created by concentrated economic and political power, not by scarcity. Resources and decision making are in the hands of a wealthy few, depriving the majority of land and jobs, and therefore of food.

Hailed by *The New York Times* as "one of the most established food think tanks in the country," Food First has grown to profoundly shape the debate about hunger and development.

But Food First is more than a think tank. Through books, reports, videos, media, and public speaking, Food First experts not only reveal the often hidden roots of hunger, they show how individuals can get involved in bringing an end to hunger. Food First inspires action by bringing to light the efforts of people and their organizations around the world who are creating farming and food systems that truly meet people's needs.

MORE BOOKS FROM FOOD FIRST

Campesino a Campesino: *Voices from Latin America's Farmer to Farmer Movement for Sustainable Agriculture*
Eric Holt-Giménez

> The voices and stories of dozens of farmers are captured in this first written history of the farmer-to-farmer movement, which describes the social, political, economic, and environmental circumstances that shape it.
> Paperback, $19.95

Promised Land: *Competing Visions of Agrarian Reform*
Edited by Peter Rosset, Raj Patel, and Michael Courville

> Agrarian reform is back at the center of the national and rural development debate. The essays in this volume critically analyze a wide range of competing visions of land reform.
> Paperback, $21.95

Sustainable Agriculture and Resistance: *Transforming Food Production in Cuba*
Edited by Fernando Funes, Luis García, Martin Bourque, Nilda Pérez, and Peter Rosset

> Unable to import food or farm chemicals and machines in the wake of the Soviet bloc's collapse and a tightening US embargo, Cuba turned toward sustainable agriculture, organic farming, urban gardens, and other techniques to secure its food supply. This book gives details of that remarkable achievement.
> Paperback, $18.95

The Future in the Balance: *Essays on Globalization and Resistance*
Walden Bello. Edited with a preface by Anuradha Mittal

> A collection of essays by global south activist and scholar Walden Bello on the myths of development as prescribed by the World Trade Organization and other institutions, and the possibility of another world based on fairness and justice.
> Paperback, $13.95

Views from the South: *The Effects of Globalization and the WTO on Third World Countries*
Foreword by Jerry Mander. Afterword by Anuradha Mittal
Edited by Sarah Anderson
> This rare collection of essays by activists and scholars from the global south describes, in pointed detail, the effects of the WTO and other Bretton Woods institutions.
> Paperback, $12.95

Basta! Land and the Zapatista Rebellion in Chiapas, Third Edition
George A. Collier with Elizabeth Lowery-Quaratiello
Foreword by Peter Rosset
> The classic on the Zapatistas in its third edition, including a preface by Rodolfo Stavenhagen.
> Paperback, $16.95

America Needs Human Rights
Edited by Anuradha Mittal and Peter Rosset
> This anthology includes writings on understanding human rights, poverty and welfare reform in America.
> Paperback, $13.95

The Paradox of Plenty: *Hunger in a Bountiful World*
Edited by Douglas H. Boucher
> Excerpts from Food First's best writings on world hunger and what we can do to change it.
> Paperback, $18.95

Education for Action: *Undergraduate and Graduate Programs that Focus on Social Change,* Fourth Edition
Edited by Joan Powell
> An updated authoritative and easy-to-use guidebook that provides information on progressive programs in a wide variety of fields.
> Paperback, $12.95

We encourage you to buy Food First Books from your local independent bookseller; if they don't have them in stock, they can usually order them for you fast. To find an independent bookseller in your area, go to *www.booksense.com*.

Food First books are also available through major online booksellers (Powell's, Amazon, and Barnes and Noble), and through the Food First website, *www.foodfirst.org*. You can also order direct from our distributor, Perseus Distribution, at (800) 343-4499. If you have trouble locating a Food First title, write, call, or e-mail us:

FOOD FIRST
398 60th Street
Oakland, CA 94618-1212 USA
Tel: (510) 654-4400
Fax: (510) 654-4551
E-mail: foodfirst@foodfirst.org
Web: www.foodfirst.org

If you are a bookseller or other reseller, contact our distributor, Perseus Distribution, at (800) 343-4499, to order.

FILMS FROM FOOD FIRST

The Greening of Cuba
Jaime Kibben

A profiling of Cuban farmers and scientists working to reinvent a sustainable agriculture based on ecological principles and local knowledge.
DVD (In Spanish with English subtitles), $35.00

America Needs Human Rights

A film told in the voices of welfare mothers, homeless men and women, low-wage workers, seniors, veterans, and health care workers.
DVD, $19.95

HOW TO BECOME A MEMBER OR INTERN OF FOOD FIRST

Join Food First

Private contributions and membership gifts fund the core of Food First/Institute for Food and Development Policy's work. Each member strengthens Food First's efforts to change a hungry world. We invite you to join Food First. As a member you will receive a 20 percent discount on all Food First books. You will also receive our quarterly publications, *Food First News and Views* and *Backgrounders*, providing information for action on current food and hunger crises in the United States and around the world. If you want to subscribe to our Internet newsletter, *People Putting Food First*, send us an e-mail at *foodfirst@foodfirst.org*. All contributions are tax-deductible.

You are also invited to give a gift membership to others interested in the fight to end hunger.

Become an Intern for Food First

There are opportunities for interns in research, advocacy, campaigning, publishing, computers, media, and publicity at Food First. Our interns come from around the world. They are a vital part of the organization and make the work possible.

To become a member or apply to become an intern, just call, visit our website, or clip and return the attached coupon to:

FOOD FIRST
398 60th Street
Oakland, CA 94618-1212 USA
Tel: (510) 654-4400
Fax: (510) 654-4551
E-mail: foodfirst@foodfirst.org
Web: www.foodfirst.org

JOINING FOOD FIRST

❏ I want to join Food First and receive a 20% discount on this and all subsequent orders. Enclosed is my tax-deductible contribution of:

❏ $25 Low Income   ❏ $50 Member   ❏ $100 Sustainer
❏ $1,000 Major Donor   ❏ OTHER

NAME _____

ADDRESS _____

CITY/STATE/ZIP _____

DAYTIME PHONE (_____) _____

E-MAIL _____

ORDERING FOOD FIRST MATERIALS

ITEM DESCRIPTION	QTY	UNIT COST	TOTAL

MEMBER DISCOUNT 20%	$ _____
CA RESIDENTS SALES TAX 8.75%	$ _____
SUBTOTAL	$ _____

PAYMENT METHOD

❏ CHECK

❏ MONEY ORDER

MAKE CHECK OR MONEY ORDER PAYABLE TO **FOOD FIRST**

❏ MASTERCARD

❏ VISA

❏ AMERICAN EXPRESS

SHIPPING DOMESTIC ORDERS: $5 FOR THE FIRST BOOK	$ _____
($2.50 FOR EACH ADDITIONAL BOOK)	$ _____
SHIPPING INTERNATIONAL ORDERS: $12 FOR THE FIRST BOOK	$ _____
($6 FOR EACH ADDITIONAL BOOK)	$ _____
MEMBERSHIP(S)	$ _____
ADDITIONAL CONTRIBUTION	$ _____
TOTAL ENCLOSED	$ _____

NAME ON CARD _____

CARD NUMBER _____ EXP. DATE _____

SIGNATURE _____

FOOD FIRST • 398 60TH STREET, OAKLAND, CA 94618-1212

For gift memberships and mailings, please see coupon on reverse side.

FOOD FIRST GIFT BOOKS

Please send a gift book to (order form on reverse side):

NAME _____

ADDRESS _____

CITY/STATE/ZIP _____

FROM _____

FOOD FIRST PUBLICATIONS CATALOGS

Please send a publications catalog to:

NAME _____

ADDRESS _____

CITY/STATE/ZIP _____

FROM _____

NAME _____

ADDRESS _____

CITY/STATE/ZIP _____

NAME _____

ADDRESS _____

CITY/STATE/ZIP _____

FOOD FIRST GIFT MEMBERSHIPS

❏ Enclosed is my tax-deductible contribution of:

❏ $50   ❏ $100   ❏ $1,000   ❏ OTHER

Please send a Food First membership to:

NAME _____

ADDRESS _____

CITY/STATE/ZIP _____

FROM _____